Snowman

R. J. Keeler

Manor House

Cataloguing Information

Keeler, Robert, J.

Snowman

(Poetry)

ISBN: 978-1-988058-56-6 (softcover)

ISBN: 978-1-988058-57-3 (hardcover)

I. Title

PS8631.R396P35 2020 C811'.6 C2020-906208-8

Copyright 2020-6-15
R. J. Keeler and Manor House publishing Inc.

Published September 15, 2020
By Manor House Publishing Inc.
452 Cottingham Crescent, Ancaster,
Ontario, Canada, L9G 3V6
905-648-4797

First Edition / 162 pages
All Rights Reserved
Cover Design: Michael Davie, Manor House
Cover Art: LilKar / Shutterstock

Snowman / R. J. Keeler

For Gracie, Miko, Rags, Avispa, Chato, Peggy, Brandy, Baylin, Bubitz, Muffy, Lizzie, Budd, Muriel, Kathy, Jim, Gale, Michiko, Mike, Isadora.

Snowman / R. J. Keeler

Table of Contents

Acknowledgements	11

First Part: Death   13

Airlock	15
If You Feel You Heal	16
The Right of the Sun to Die	17
Thick Fog Bank over Sound—Armistice Day, November 11th	19
Death of a Horse at High Altitude	20
Snake	22
Things I Wasn't Supposed to Hear	23
Insufficient Opportunity	24
Fixing Dinner	25
Spell Check	26
Krakatoa	27
A Body Dies from Longing	28
Walking Across America	29
Pain Is Pleasure's Principle	31
In 1942, on the Bataan Death March, an American Officer Made to Kneel	32
Fork	33
Rat Me Out	34
Pan Pan Pan	35
The Blind IRS Tax Examiner	37
The Antithesis of Magic	38
On the Occasion of the Incarceration of the Assistant State Attorney General's Wife for Making over One Hundred Threatening Telephone Calls to Her Neighbor	39

Second Part: Love, et al.   41

What Is Essential in Life Must of Necessity Be Invisible   43

Begin   45

Naughty Cocklebur, Artful Iris   46

Some Observations and Reflections on Shelly in Her Tight Green Pants   48

A Sea of Boxes   50

The Arbitrager of Love   51

Radio Talk Show   52

Modesty Blaise, John Galt: A Forgotten Love Story   53

Weeding is Never Done   55

Shadow Box   56

How a Poem Is Like an Erection   57

Pirate Mailbox   58

Neanderthal Love   59

Divinity of Christ   60

The Side the Light Is Coming From   61

Miss Bonatred Looks across Her Fence   62

That Eddyline   63

Remembering Buddha   65

Requiem for John C. Holmes   66

Diary of Transits   67

Snake Medicine   68

What Ever Happened to Ursula Andress?   70

Third Part: The Natural World   71

Cold Wind of the Night   74

Thistles   75

Regarding the Futility of Operating a Noisy Leaf Blower in Mid-November	76
Nurse Log	77
Ross Dam	78
Flying the Hump	79
Signs	80
Glossolalia	81
What's a Weed and What's a Flower?	82
Stone, She	83
Rewilding	84
How to Love a Plant	85
Minimal Colors	86
Black Swan	87
Birds	89
Of Dark or Bright Forces	90
Not a Flower	91
Every year, almost about this same time,	93
The Lead Mare	94
Trust No One with Only One Oar	95
Twinned Sides	96
Don't Surrender to the Bear's Way	97
rake	98
On the Art of Sailing, Lost	99
Suppose the Rainy Season	101
Cold Rain	102
Four and a Half Haiku for Spring	103

Fourth Part: Science, Fun, Odds & Ends — 105

Oh, Make-Believe	107
Epitaph for Pre-consent Decree AT&T	108
The Twice-Born	109
Of What Use Is a Bungee Cord in a Clever Universe Full of Time?	110
Moon's Muscle Memory	115
Training Your Intuition	117
Head End Hop Off	118
The Sound of Rushing Water	119
How We Learn	120
Ode to the Syrian Arab Republic on Our Tax Day, April 17, 2018	121
Pluto Haiku	122
Dark Abstraction	123
Spirit Level	125
Doxology	127
22 Reasons Why There Is Such Widespread Emphasis on Zombies These Days	129
Regarding a Recent Call from Heather in Account Services	130
A Long Residential Sadness	131

Last Part: Literature — 133

Meaning Has No Matter outside of Sound	135
W	136
Calling Something by a Different Name	137
Base Flow, Drought Flow	138
Kicked to the Curb	139
Prey Drive as Metaphor	140
See What Happens	141

Plato's Cave Redux	143
The Only Color of White	144
On Receiving an Author's First Book of Poems	145
There Are No Found Poems, Just Found Rags, Bones	146
Unknown Unknowns	147
Curtains of White	149
The First Horse	151
(The high moral tone)	152
We Must Pray the Prayer That Knows No Words	153
Habitude	154
Nemawashi	155
Oh, That Heartstrike	156
Notes	157
About the Author	161

Snowman / R. J. Keeler

Acknowledgements

I would like to thank the editors of the following journals and presses who first printed or selected these poems:

- *Arlington Literary Journal (ArLiJo)*: "Requiem for John C. Holmes" (forthcoming 2020)
- *Blueline Magazine*: "Cold Rain"
- *Broad River Review*: "Fork"
- *California State Poetry Society, 2019 Annual Poetry Contest, 1st Prize*: "Stone, She"
- *Camas*: "Suppose the Rainy Season"
- *Cathexis Northwest Press*: "Signs"
- *Crosswinds Poetry Journal*: "The Side the Light Is Coming From"
- *Curating Alexandria*: "Snake" and "The First Horse"
- *Elmbridge Literary Competition*: "Every year, almost about this same time,"
- *Friends Bulletin*: "rake" (first published as "I Want to Wring the Day of Song") and "Thistles"
- *Griffith Review's Crimes and Punishments*: "Pirate Mailbox"
- *Grindstone Literary 2019 International Poetry Prize Shortlist*: "Radio Talk Show," 2020 yearly anthology
- *Indolent Books*: "Meaning Has No Matter Outside Sound"
- *Lotus-eater*: "The Blind IRS Tax Examiner"
- *Ottawa Arts Review*: "Habitude" (published as "Dream-Lines")
- *PCC Inscape Magazine*: "Divinity of Christ"
- *Piece Magazine*: "On the Occasion of the Incarceration of the Assistant State Attorney General's Wife for Making over One Hundred Threatening Telephone Calls to Her Neighbor"
- *North Carolina Poetry Society, Pinesong Awards Anthology*: "Naughty Cocklebur, Artful Iris"
- *Rue Scribe*: "(The high moral tone)"
- *Secret Lunar Wars Anthology*: "Moon's Muscle Memory" (forthcoming 2021)
- *Talking Writing*: "The Right of the Sun to Die" (forthcoming 2020)
- *Terror House Magazine*: "Nurse Log" and "Observations and Reflections on Shelly in Tight Green Pants"
- *The American Journal of Poetry*: "Dark Abstraction"

- *The Criterion*: "Begin"
- *The Dreamers Creative Writing*: "Bonsai" (the fourth haiku in "Four and a Half Haiku for Spring")
- *The Menteur*: "Trust No One with Only One Oar"
- *The Reach of Song,* Georgia Poetry Society's annual anthology: "What Ever Happened to Ursula Andress?"
- *The Transnational*: "22 Reasons Why There Is such Widespread Emphasis on Zombies these Days"
- *Tight Magazine*: "Minimal Colors"
- *Wild Words Summer Solstice Competition 2019*: "Prey Drive as Metaphor" (highly commended but not published)
- *Wingless Dreamer Poetry Contest*: "How We Learn"
- *Writing for Peace's DoveTales*: "How to Love a Plant"

The author wishes to thank Manor House Publishing and its founder Michael B. Davie for selecting this manuscript for publication.

Thanks also to a long line of teachers, mentors, and fellow students, including Guy Owen, Jim Heynen, Jana Harris, David Wagoner, David Whyte, Matt Briggs, Belle Randall, Richard Kenney, Linda Bierds, Christianne Balk, Jan Wallace, Jane Hirshfield, Nikolai Popov, Susan Lynch, and most especially Heather McHugh.

This work inspired in part by the late poet John Lawrence Ashbery, who wished his work to be accessible to as many people as possible and not to be a private dialogue with himself

First Part: Death

Snowman / R. J. Keeler

Airlock

> "Cause a pressure drop, oh pressure
> Oh yeah pressure gonna drop on you"
> — Jimmy Cliff, in his last film, *The Harder They Come*

First a door, then sundry vestibules in between, then an outer door.
Take your time, but please do pass on through.

The infant Darwin and the baby Orca
each in turn open then step across—step inside—
their own first door
to inhabit, for their own varied run or term,
a considerable vestibule:
maybe wide or short, maybe narrow, maybe brightly
colored or, worse, muted and dull.

Then, like torrid energy, like after what seemed a split second,
there is an unfamiliar surging in and out,
either bumpy or like quelled plate glass,
but sometimes splashed crosswise by bile and fires.

Pause, you, just a moment in that middle; savor your far-off but
oncoming quiet.
When ready, take yourself near to the second threshold
and obtain from chaos into absolute stillness.

Don't hold back now,
there is no reverse path.

Dive for that outer door
then fly out.

If You Feel You Heal

> Not for the first time, Seaweed Greaser kills off his son, Larry, who's then revived by pimp-messiah Jessy, twice incanting, "If you feel you heal!" —from Robert Downey Sr.'s 1972 Western, *Greaser's Palace*.

Children and women, mon chéri,
precede the crew. Oh, what crew:
junior engineer, second mate, and
two captains—both bipolar, both
absolute, ragged buttholes. Each
delivers cant, blowhardness, white
lies, slatherings-on to calm the swaying
life-raft throngs. No survivor guilt
here—all go down or none go down.
Apart sits ship's chief engineer, cryptic
Nigerian Igbo medicine man, Ikenga!

    Your sacred Igbo name is *place of strength*.
    Your deity, Alusi, speaks: *Ikenga, can*
    you now wrestle in this land of the dead?

Women, children, crew turn, say: *Conjure*
us a holy juju, Ikenga; fix this unsettlement.
Go below, fetch from hiding and consecrate
your Statue of Victory; chant artful words:

    Mawu-Lisa, Ikengam kwalu
    otu, njee mge ona mmuo

The Right of the Sun to Die

The right of the pear tree to bear pear fruit
And the right of the apple tree to bear apple fruit
And the right of the Italian plum tree to bear plums
The right of the crows to eat the pear and apple and delicious plums
And then drop the partially eaten fruit on the earth below
And the right of ants and roly-bugs—wood lice—to clean the dropped pear or apple or plum seeds of any remaining fruit
And of wild ground bees to clean the dropped seeds of any remaining fruit
Then the right of the true hawk or kestrel or even the eagle to raid the crows' nests and lance and eat the near-featherless squabs, even the right to kill the parent crows
Then drop the partially eaten crow corpses on the ground below or on the water of shallow, brackish bays
Then the right of harbor crabs or earthworms to strip the squabs' bones of flesh
Then the right of earthworms, after stripping the squabs' bones, to methodically go back and cultivate the soil beneath the apple, pear, and plum trees
And the right of fly larvae to reprise the picking of twice-cleaned bones to make them evenly clean
And the right of the sun to die
After it exercises its right to swell to a red giant and incinerate the younger earth
And incinerate all the inner planets
And incinerate all known life: fruit trees, hawks, earthworms, roly-bugs, crabs, bees
Then the right of remnant dust after the destruction of the sun and solar system
And eventually the right of all suns in the galaxy to die, become dust, or bear fruit
And the right of the entire Milky Way to either die or bear fruit
And the right of trillions of galaxies to swell up and either bear fruit or die
And the right of bugs and other sentients to predict these swellings and deaths and bearings of fruit and suns and of final light
And not to have any right to return things to square zero or to kick over the game board
Or to despise, however incidentally, the movie as it plays, start to end,

frame by frame
Only the right to change the reels as they are shown and consumed, one after another
Or if astronomically lucky, the right to splice the film as it breaks and the movie stops
and the house lights come back on momentarily

Thick Fog Bank over Sound—Armistice Day, November 11th

Dismayed, except flounders who couldn't see
or care. Predictions were all wrong, as usual,
so muted angst not surprising. Hydraulic pump-
motor oilers laze, smoke, and deal Go Fish.

St. Matthew Passion swells; diminished sevenths
convey Jesus' prophecies. Pontius Pilate
reluctantly condemns to death. The Chief
Mate revels, sways, and dips; she's distracted,

preoccupied. But cold steel truth obtains:
no two vessels can, in space or time, coexist.
Predictions were all wrong, of course. No
white light—just stunned feeling of compression.

Death of a Horse at High Altitude

The epoch after the shot
bringing the gifted horse
to drift slightly upward,
toward the overhead fluted, air duct.
Bringing the gifted horse
to seem to want to hang tipped in
space a bit
as if he were squinting;
the shadow of the raised arm
of the hired veterinarian blackening
the fuselage's
far opposite bulkhead.

The pilot in the cockpit of
the chartered air cargo radioing
the emergency guard frequency
circled
and lifted off his map—his seatbelt
cinched tight
across his tense stomach.

The copilot's altitude gauge
unwinding anticlockwise; its larger hand
syncopated, whipping across the
smaller, luminous inner hand.

Muted crests of a ragged
divide right below; far ahead,
the land brightly sheened, with blunt
snow massing;
a rising, soft pink light out to the east,
so encouraging.

Way out in front, past the high,
visible eastern curve, a mile-and-a-half
course of Bermuda grass; hand-manicured,
green, cool, untrampled, not yet
withstanding handicaps.

Snowman / R. J. Keeler

The gifted racehorse panicking—
night or turbulence or neither;
the nylon restraints
loose or ill-knotted; the belts
undersized.

The emergency medical kit
opened; a single-shot pistol
fumbled, then grasped firmly.

The daughter toward the back
of the leased air transport
bringing her hands over her ears.

Snake

Cold, lifeless reptile, who can defend you?
Silent sliver of God's making, self-possessed
beyond human ken—What did you say?
Eve? Oh, wasn't she such a chatterer?
No wonder, at end, your apple went into her mouth;
anything, just to be able
to hear clearly again God's
fat mice scraping at the delicate
dirt of the
Garden.

You lie there, snake,
vulnerable but deadly, a cited handmaiden
to that old, late-conflicted Maker of your old, divided line;
who cast out and uplifted, who created everything,
but in everything created flaws.

You lie there, snake,
between hammering sky and ancient hell, yammering
like an invisible ventriloquist,
in black-striped, red-striped, green or yellow livery
waiting for me
to pass
close.

Things I Wasn't Supposed to Hear

At first there was the clamor, next came feelings.
No songbirds now; no whippoorwills shall ever
sound an occasional pain, or hover,
or warble at last across their fray's areal.

Sounds that only dogs should heed aloud—
that hissing bullet that killed my grandfather;
that tinkling as my life flashed across my eyes;
outside my barred windows, a big cat's cough.

Annapurna sings her left-handed mistral;
confidentiality becomes abysmal
for the mailman's private missal.
I've yet to hear the stars' winged kestrel.

In the back yard there is a deep well;
throw me down it when I falter, as I will.

Insufficient Opportunity

Every drop of snowy rain soaks bare-black earth;
layers of scattered, secretive, loamy fingers point
up; dazed, compact clouds point down—nothing
in between to catch their fall. So considerate, faith!

Eyelashes sweep out dance-arcs; they mark unreal
parts of sense, of whiffs of reason, of gentle torque
into unpredicted universes—*Oh, may all be well*.
We have so little space and time in which to mark

a brightened point apart; while, down below, under
tender, holy skins, overburdening us all, a tranche—
wild and squirming with success, joy, inner dance,
fish, and mostly wonderful and intimate thunder.

Who walks about? Speak truth, all Diogenes out there.
A minor instant on our great arc-path from antiquity;
we fuss with frippery throughout our term; so, where
do I, we, go to find surprising, amenable propinquity?

Face-first with a sudden singularity, try not to so beam;
and never make to cross deep chasms in two itsy jumps.
Certainly, many awkward inconsistencies and bumps
could result if you launch failing a full head of steam.

Until we hear the toothsome clarion, *All Boats Away;*
consider—in universes writ large, there are no bad liars.
In *Sands of the Kalahari*, as baboons encircle their prey,
O'Brien's knell opines, *Life is irresistible, tickets do expire*.

Alleluia! Why not bust open twenty river-smooth rocks
into lumpy parts, then let's locate their homeboy quasars.
What's infused deep in those hunks of burned-out stars?
A soft, lovely interference: hums, wild squirrels, copses.

Fixing Dinner

She ran cool water from the faucet over red bell peppers, turning each with her left hand as she cradled them in her right. After cleaning the third pepper, she picked up a zucchini and started to clean it. She felt the skin, rough with tiny prickles. Behind her, at their gas stove, she heard his water boiling. *The skin is almost prickly,* she said softly.

As he faced the old gas stove, he gently stirred pasta into boiling water. He felt content and mildly happy. It had been a good day for them. They had worked together in the garden all afternoon; only once, when he let the watering can fall onto some starts, had she snapped at him. He was quite hungry; he felt also that different kind of hunger. He glanced slyly over his shoulder at her long, sloping back.

Son and daughter-in-law, daughter-in-law and son. They were a good team, both tall and fit and absorbed in fixing their evening meal. The father wondered, as he sat quietly at their side, what they thought of him; when they were alone, did they discuss what to do with him if, or when, he became too aged?

In two minutes, I'll be ready to throw in your veggies, he said to her.

OK, she responded, *two minutes.* She finished with the last zucchini, pushed it off the cutting board's side, and picked up her long, sharp knife.

Spell Check

Mumbo-jumbo, tail of newt;
   left hand out for bread
   and loot—what you conceal
   versus what you reveal.

All over back lots at Majdanek, spell-
   makers waved their striped wands and
   stood, flashlights in hand, late into night
   around consecrated spell books; whipped

pages back and forth, pointed here and there
   with fashionably lacquered fingernails;
   to contest some point of lore or cite
   a dusty footnote or a futile reference.

I'd wish they'd suffer a florid anti-Holocaust
   time-warp spell on all those Bergen-Belsen
   barracks guards walking home, after shift,
   to pet and curry their fawning family dog.

Then be not there, Prometheus—you dodged and swerved
   lest you be tortured, were lifted up, only to be retortured.
   Once you sent us, quite in sympathy, Zeus's past-stolen fires,
   but myths forewent; today, in sodden camps, hollow fires
   don't serve to just warm starved deviants or undesirables.

Krakatoa

Pele's mercy conflicts a robed choir
that chants, *No mercy, quarter—nor forgiveness*.
But to thread the needle's prompt, to be
inside the Krakatoa that very instant

of loose surprise, when time runs mostly backwards
and all else pales—even Saladins
fret about fallout spewed far
from the cauldron's high board.

A turned-inside-out, simmering
keyhole, dull ochre like Yellowstone,
shunts triage aside and cracks the case—
the Big Guy smirks and lifts his august eyebrow.

Why will wife cook eggs that summer morning?
Why will husband bike to work that summer morning?

A Body Dies from Longing

His furred cat lounges master-
less. Buried so deep within
ripe vines, no one apart
noticed a final movement—
was there ever one? Thorned
bricklayer's fingers, stiffened
at yesterday, pointed out
to an old cannery's crumbled
smokestack—once a cone-
shaped, handmade seashell;
once fastened, brick by brick,
over a century ago with
Chincoteague horsehair
and mercury folded
inside solid, wet mortar.

The cave-in, traced to
tired ironworkers' blunders—
eleven hoop-iron fasteners
ill-augured, bent, weak—
last week destroyed his
union labor work crew.
Each workmen's fragile brow
compressed to chalk—femurs
interlaced with sunny bricks—
as he, at his office desk,
compiled yearly pension costs.

Over-numbed by reports of
his crushed and buried crew,
he flipped his family's farmland,
turning it back to oncoming
winter fallow; fitful, stumbled
down to blindly burrow
deep inside the black belly
of blackberry brambles.

Walking Across America

By consolidating all dignity
   into my left pocket, last week I
   walked all across America.

Then last night
   I walked all the way back to my
   starting point. Dignity, and all my
   frail nobility, came to mind,
   but somewhat faintly.

I never do speculate
   that death or others are coming for me;
   after all, what counts most—an external world
   that is bounded, never limitless—or
   an internal world, uncountable,
   almost certainly infinite?

So, death is not just some slow greening;
   rather is a quietly ceasing to exist.
   Death, considerately without feature or destination, asks only,
   Where to?
   And all this time I have been alone
   and walking.

If I'm walking but can't understand where I'm headed,
   is there no destination? Or perhaps this journey is only
   about wholly crystalline trust.

It's not too late for me to turn again, to backtrack?

I could have seen everything outside as something
   simply called geometry.
   Is there no adequate bulwark between these two slices,
   no hopscotching?

So much of our world is based on oddity, boundary—differentiation.
   Aren't there any soft edges or outlines, ahead or behind?
   Why then walk? What's the point of this
   or anything?

Snowman / R. J. Keeler

Here is my own case for orthogonality:
   If all things are green, why does it matter
   to think only of colorlessness? Any stark schism
   is not both an exterior and an interior.
   And I'm still walking to unknowns.

But any one step, out or back, invests action and energy—
   such a post-green revolt must presume one
   surrounding object.

What could I see if everything is simply solid green?
   Green's so arbitrary; color matters nil so long as there
   are no other shaded colors.

Pain Is Pleasure's Principle

The half-guarded night
turns to leave a forest.

Rain attacks the far edge,
crushes ferns,
bursts swollen pods,

drives seeds
through mud and earth.

Moon clouds steel
unruly fog.

Pleasure is pain's passion.

Snowman / R. J. Keeler

In 1942, on the Bataan Death March, an American Officer Made to Kneel

sword scrapes wood scabbard
neck waits, time drifts—mountain fog?
white blindfold flies up

Fork

Sullen heat lightning forks and bends down
to spike earth, forks then forks then pounds
a wanton-exposed ground. Forks, like silver,
shatter whole cloth, and, to be candid, split

rod into cleft. A fork, a single one, is a wild, bitter
place in which to be—a salt tributary, all hitlered.
Were limbs to turn to hinge in hard time, each fork
might devise its final no-going-back place, its clock.

The RR junction switch wrenched left, then nearly
instantly again back right. Two lines of queerly
ladened boxcars diverge; all wave fond farewell.
In just a few minutiae, memories fork or pale;

so let them be spit out. Then, microscopically lost
one-siders turn aside, go into gardens, cut dark,
secret flowers from wet-acid bowers, arrange
into cameral chambers of porcelain hearts; gain,

like lean, ex-nihilo veins under skin, some tangle.
Tree branches, forked into dirt, move the needles.
Time slows for both limbs of *any* forked path;
each limb diminishes the whole body's wrath.

Tangled fields fade away, squash the tyranny
of one single track; both cabooses' lights dizzily
distance out; their path is a stark abandonment,
each from the other. Any fork is an awful ardent

instrument of evil, like a red-hot metal knife blade.
The trodden path is greener—and so do not be afraid.

Rat Me Out

Frack this holy ground
it can bear no weight;
no constitution at hand
to assuage our guilt.

But use a bigger ratchet-
wrench—whatever helps
to hold back that surging
tide of stony, evil books.

This late winter after-
noon, come any flood—
after a hopeful respite
the waters of blood

toss over all sand, hat-
bands, flowered capes;
we are all always con-
scripted by our edges.

So rat me out, tell me
things I must never know.
Your feint of hands and
minds—ever slow, slow.

Grasshoppers intrude
far onto our workbench;
how can this, so weak,
be forceful all at once?

Rat me out you big-
hearted Judas, send me
canny flowers, else—will
I cave? Or cop a plea?

Pan Pan Pan

Three of anything—
hearts or stars, even bones.
Bricks or campfires, even limbs—
make a signal
for distress,
for assistance, succor.

Three crossed trees
on new-blown snow:
Rescue me, please.
Three open hearts
in a row: *love you*'s
in astral competition.
Bird, Bird, Bird may
always be random,
or be tomorrow's hope
for clear, buoyant skies.

So go on foot now along
the very edge of a cliff,
but skirt it. *Pay attention,*
said Socrates, or you might
entangle signals like these
threes: Olympic medals,
wishes, or Cerberus heads.

There was nothing in today's
newspaper to lend concern.
The benevolent orders of
several endangered animals
put their thumbs collectively
on the scales.

Any volta of sorts is referred
to as a state of urgency.
Maybe cornered by hungry bears.
Maybe had to duck into an ice-cave
with no provisions at hand.

Snowman / R. J. Keeler

Three stars: one very bright,
one a comet, one a planet.
I have this image in mind
of a snow-covered mountain.

The Blind IRS Tax Examiner

At my recent federal audit
the blind IRS tax examiner
demands a specific receipt
from my document box—
detailing our business travel
to and from home and work.
He whips it out of my left hand
and thrusts it into
his high-powered, brilliantly lighted
magnifying device.

Fifty thousand years ago
his precious flawed
body would have been
explicitly left out
at night
as a gift
for marauding predatory cats.

And, of course, genus
Homo didn't have any
income tax back then
or really anything
except fear and hunger
darkness and vermin.

So, perhaps the blind IRS tax examiner's
high-powered, brilliantly lighted
magnifying device
could have helped
those *Homo*s at dusk
to start their cooking fires,
or to examine their skins for lice,
or even assist some schoolchildren
to finish their algebra homework.

Snowman / R. J. Keeler

The Antithesis of Magic
      —in memoriam, the Karlowitz family

Blazing sleights of hand undergird a faked decapitation;
    white rabbits graze intermittently inside a top hat;
    sour water seeps into the locked safe, where, within,
    Houdini sits to devour his pastrami on rye.

Two young men, Gale and Jim—I knew them both—died in some past,
    unholy era. Died, not befriended by mucky pools—asphyxiated
    out from flesh. Each had sat in my Philosophy of Relativism class.

Decades later, I learned every last, lost detail:
    what each read on their last night; did they
    enjoy life, or visit Mount Athos, or even the Vatican,
    prior to floating off into their soupy bouquet?

Ionized, low-pH, ombrotrophic water evacuates eyes and barnacles, tars
    everything mossy brown. All factions, apart Gale and Jim—and one
    other unblessed, suicidal, middle-aged female—seem happy with
    magic.

The Navy subbase recruits, ordered to beat swamps, found
    that middle-aged woman late in quiet, evening sun: facedown,
    blue arms out akimbo, in a reedy, backlot marsh.
    We circled her, stood around; guessed she'd stolen

out a nearby home, not planned to return. I recall, fifty years later,
    spent cigarette butts strewn atop marsh reeds; her splayed-out blue
    blouse. But stage magic seemingly follows a separate, kinder, more
    patient track—

two delicate, quick hands fan a blue-gold scarf
    and then, in a puff of smoke, a stage brunette turns
    into a braying donkey. But three just-minted souls,
    immersed and laden in steamy liquid swirls, don't.

On the Occasion of the Incarceration of the Assistant State Attorney General's Wife for Making over One Hundred Threatening Telephone Calls to Her Neighbor

These are the shards:
a chilly climate, a heaving breast;
her calamity, her fertile disaster.
Once,
she did command a magnificent vessel.

Cast down
by some hideous strength, by some ouroborian worm
that infiltrated reason, sowed piles of transparent scats,

perhaps she was so thirsty for life,
she fell into that ugly maelstrom
then became progressively thirsty for plight.

We are all cast down a hundred times
in life by forces
older than amber.
We are all pinned against cold green foams of our own making.

In dense, remote Amazonian rainforest jungles, lightning-lit
fires burn for weeks
unseen by white man.
One hundred thousand hectares of old trees ablated: underbrush, early
growth, gone—sane acts of Providence.

In dry season, however, those low fires burn
for months, trickling into furrows, bypassing ridges. Why and when
did her conspiring genius, like green folds of winter cabbage,
turn arcanely malevolent?

Over time, stands of young juniper and mango trees rise up again.

Snowman / R. J. Keeler

Second Part: Love, et al.

Snowman / R. J. Keeler

What Is Essential in Life Must of Necessity Be Invisible

Pain, one thing we have no shortage of,
or of a beloved dog's unconditional love.
So say amen and amass more, build more.
Say amen, and do not delay.

Like any visible but inessential symbol,
like any awkward natural wonder—example,
a local waterfall, recently dolled up
by overhormonal, golf-playing bipeds;

its cold stream-water whistles down
a wet face to smash a lower holding pool
where circling Chinook love nanoscopic,
aerated bubbles and stirred up macrophytes.

But what energizes this wondrous, exacting
frenzy? Any local native may obtain real
objectiveness, close and hard, in hand
or mind, but when some friend later seeks

to remove it—when, like liquid helium,
it just slides through fingers—
then it's all so pyrrhic and impositive.

But, gentlepeople, to bring a necessary
essence—most invisible, like those salmons'
certain love, or their abundant hunger, or like

a perfect but tiny, half-visible, aerated bubble—
to bring such frailty into our formidably
visible world instantly exposes each

well-conscripted wisp to vast, punishing,
and roustabouted rudeness. So, is necessity's

lack of lack a recent, somewhat-twisted story
made up to dis-entertain? Life usually queers

up all such scenarios—double-cross

Snowman / R. J. Keeler

what can be accessed, pinball the rest?

These tender stories may never loop
newborn infants out to Pluto.

Begin

Birthed like some now-cold stone,
I am descendant from lyrical fire,
from rhapsody—then quenched down.

Female lava ripples over male; seawater's
cold sucks out each heated pulse.
Congealed—a crow's-wing black rafter

hanging boiled ocean over coarse,
winged bottom-sand. So I begin:
homologous. Unlike random eddies

in the deep Marianas Trench, I can
let kin's blood with any random feint.
The just-woven net—I throw it. I troll

the ocean's green.

Naughty Cocklebur, Artful Iris

Damn! Sand in my shoes and on my left sleeve
a rabid cocklebur with stem. I'll bet this prickly object
latched on when my coat pillowed our recent tryst.
Well, inside my vase sit last night's mementos—two bright irises.
Rough bur lying with smooth flower: an echo of old rites: man praising
woman. Oh, we've drifted out to sea so far, so fast; I only meant to
charm.

What's the essence—my God!—of her bewitching charm?
When we're apart, my heart's long out on my sleeve,
and for a lovely gutter worm I have more praise
than for that singular moon. Apart, I'm keen for rovers who'd object
their deftness onto her, who'd sing, *What hair. . so soft. . my lovely Iris*.
Don't heed them, please. You'll be most rewarded at our coming tryst.

Damn all women—and her! At first, with purest thoughts, they tryst
a man's gentle, lamblike nature, but when they commence to charm,
with sighs and perfumed hands, his iris
swells to match the girth of mighty Bunyan's sleeve.
Then his nature changes; intentions veer to base. No wonder they
object;
in woman's mind, it was purely his design. In penance, men can only
praise.

Joy, ache, joy—where does the balance rest? That I cannot praise.
Now, hooked like a dumb fish, I flounder toward tomorrow's tryst.
                              But I wonder, how goes the object
of my sweet contempt? I'll bet she lolls in some chic shop; she draws a
charm
slowly back and forth across a slender wrist, while at her sleeve
a seamstress deftly pins and shapes a cloth of many-colored iris.

Last evening, beside our bower, I knelt to wrench two yellow irises
from steaming mud. *For you,* I offered, *your blessed soul to praise*.
She reached, but, when she glanced along my arm, recoiled: *Your*
sleeve!
It's caked with muck. Go away, clean yourself; tonight will be no tryst!
I stared and choked, but then I swear she worked her charm:
her gaze went level, her lips occult, and I could no further object.

Snowman / R. J. Keeler

Balls! Just to hurl this wretched vase against a nearby stony object!
The bur, of course, would fall; the blow would smash her pale irises.
Calm, calm! She'd be so . . . startled, she might withhold her youthful
                                                                                              charms.
      Last night, after—so blissful. She kissed me, whispered, *Praise
our earthborn bodies. Heaven's not for us, dear; it frowns upon such
                                                                                               trysts.*
She leaned to me, raised her mouth; her hand pulled down my sleeve.

Rough cocklebur lying along smooth iris; a charm, a talisman, to praise
our love and bind us close? Well, hell! Tonight, for sure, another tryst;
my only object there, to savor a deeper consolation of her tender sleeve.

Some Observations and Reflections on Shelly in Her Tight Green Pants

*—Since green pants are colorful and draw the eye,
the rest of the outfit is often conservative.*

This morning I observed
a two-way ant-bridge along
a narrow twig, overflowing
with rushing, black ant-soldiers.

Those ant-soldiers, although
not mindless, may be feckless
and shorn; so, pray tell: exactly
why and how frantic ants
reflect on a young women's
tight green pants?

Oh, ants may always wander out
to find green things—leaves or blades—
saw them into tiny chunks, then
grasp them with pincers and scurry
back to home's nest. And what if ants
were to decide to delicately
attack Shelly, to pull and cut at
her green outer-garments?

> *Color blocking is the fashion*
> *practice of wearing two bold*
> *colors in big blocks. In this*
> *case, match the green pants*
> *with another bold color*
> *on top, such as melon or yellow.*

Overall, when I last saw her,
I thought Shelly seemed
very kicky and upturned
with tons of imposed attitude.

> *Constant hope encircles, but*
> *exactly how to grab green*
> *before it tints to moderate?*

Snowman / R. J. Keeler

> *White/grey/black, a long way*
> *to go for daft postal illumination.*
> *Leave the obvious*
> *comment for the end.*

Rather, the jacket she wore
over the green pants was
elegant—black/white
and sparkling—just perfect.

> *Color is magical. It has the power*
> *to soothe, energize, and can even*
> *have a healing effect. Being surrounded*
> *by colors we love in our lives*
> *makes us happier.*

I keep debating her pants' relative
hue of green. But I *don't* recall
what color shoes she was wearing.

A green planet's excesses of color,
chlorophyll in all the earth's cracks,
then two slender legs, whatever.

A Sea of Boxes

i. Along the shore weave and bob—
tilt, flash—a twisting grayness,
a just-massed, fog-like bank. Grab
those few bobbing at water's edge,

open one or two, or all—see?
Each box is empty; it gapes like an
angry viper's mouth—just vacant!
What's missing inside that flotilla

of cardboard cartons? Could an empty
box, in contradiction, conceal our knacks?
So scratch answers on snake hides, contrive,
suffice them into that sullen naval fleet.

ii. Impart to mind worn out travails;
pick wispy purple excesses—any
ghost of night sweats, minor love's
abundances. Pack them intact into a

quaint tiny box afloat along an occluded
transit of Jupiter. Thus do we, dry land
sailors, rearrange, repot a pecked life.
Upon that very instant, those bobbing

boxes offer deep crevasses, model us
a watery fleet of flying lanterns, gift us
vehicles for our *letting go*'s. Excepting
an unconsciousness, how else to dispel?

iii. Spend two nights in Marrakesh,
suddenly you think you know it well.

The Arbitrager of Love

flips one off for someone else far worse,
someone more horny and wild. But he's blindsided
by lust, so turns his attention away
to fall off the far end of scarlet desire,
to go undermarket or, maybe, to try again tomorrow.
No one unloved is allowed truth of bargained love.

What is to be made of he who invites harsh punishment?
Who is this unholy arbiter but to a blade of grass?
No, his god is in a kitchen cooking stew bones into soup.
He is like the collapse of the beehive,
the decline of frog's carrying capacity,
or coral reef bleaching.

Why cracks manifest in love—just outspoken fear?
Can't we just fly over valleys and dips, canyons and chasms?
From up there, everything looks whole, sealed up, healed;
the green fields shoulder against one another in full harmony.
But his feints draw life into open light and uncover
a fine line between disgust and classless equipoised love.

Radio Talk Show

Time—oh, how you conceal your cleverness   When

    the talk show host says,   *Number six, go ahead you're next*
you're in there   swinging   When the young girl says,   *Hello?*
Am I on?
you
    leap to catch the words   you twist them
on their side   What
    we hear is   *I want to find my mother   I want to come back
home again   I want*

    The talk show host says,   *Talk a little softer, you're causing
feedback*

Time, that's your signal
    You're with her   in that telephone booth   in San Jose
a   twenty-dollar bill   folded   in her torn back pocket   new
against
the skin of her unclothed ass

unshaven black whiskers scraping her lips and cheek
strained voice going   *Argh   Argh   Argh*

The talk show host asks,   *Where are you calling from?*
Richmond, she says   but he
    knows   the number
he sees it   on his console screen   He asks her   another question

But
he's asking   *you,*   Time

She tries to muffle   the freeway noise   She presses her palm
hard
    against her   right ear

That's your signal, Time

Modesty Blaise, John Galt: A Forgotten Love Story

> . . . creating a woman who, though fully feminine, would be as good in combat and action as any male. —Peter O'Donnell, *Crime Time*
> Who is John Galt? —Ayn Rand, *Atlas Shrugged*

Strong winds crosswised an empty frozen field.
Ripped and downed branches still flowered white.
There was so much time.

An exceptional young woman—
many talents but also the
inveterate criminal.

Always,
she walks her own path;

she,
a set individual throughout
all her many adventures.

She understands: cultivating a
persona only lends strength.

Focused,
resourceful, ever in humor, ever
defining her *own* fate and
fortune.

Still, but especially now,
singularly feral; governed by
morals, not law.

She thinly debates any principle
of closeness among comrades.

That man who simply loved life,
and for his unobstructed
efforts held nothing but joy.
His only song was for immense
deliverances

For him, *love*
simply meant *to value;* not
causeless love or causeless
emotion.

Love—men ought to feel this
for any such rare woman; an
expression of his intense values.

Divine to love that woman, even if
for all her flaws;

the less she may deserve it, the
more she's owed his dignity of
love.

Oh, John, our friend, how
are you so *not* human? Can you not
ever feel without first thinking?
Are you not capable of matchless
love?

When struck by feeling, why is
fear the only avenue you *can*
exactly bring to mind?

Snowman / R. J. Keeler

Does he,   Is this just pure chance,
she wonders, does he favor her?   or a matter for some present
                                          catastrophe?

The universal wheel-turners—monarchs, kings:
their ability to cut across obstacle and illusion.

A brilliant double rainbow to the west-northwest.
A great scar on the water, every way a bright scar.
A symphony of triumphs has swept space clean.

The great wheel turns and turns, then turns again.
What are women—men—to a single blade of grass?

Weeding is Never Done

Weeding is great therapy
Certainly helps the flowers
More flowers more pollen
More butterflies and bees
More flowers and fruit
More pies and punches
More parties and bars
More fondling and kisses
More doing the wild thing
More *Holy Shit*s
More contractions and pukes
More gynes and speculums
More Lamaze and waiting
More packed meals and bags
More false starts and suddenly wetted floors
More panic and craziness
More bills more insanity
Maybe time to start gardening
Maybe time to sow some seeds
Maybe time to grow some weeds

Shadow Box

Heart conscripts us all around and
there are no longer any open fields,
whereas before we could observe
a veil of occidentalism, or essences.

Heart strikes us deep, perhaps deeper;
emotions are slashed, fagots burn them.
No mercy abounding at any epicenter;
we have to put an end to senselessness.

So, join our army of lesser wingless angels,
fight with us for admiration, for invisibility.
Nothing ever changes, or sinks selectively,
or levels out onto smaller issues, or wholes.

The colorful spines of heart-transmittals
are soft but impactful. Then heart-trails
lead off to thicker woods or to far
foreign savannas. Then time splits:

one split runs away, goofy double-timing,
a second freezes until magnetism dawns.
Hadrian's wall covers the morose land,
divides it into two parts, or maybe twelve.

Heart reconstituted: a long-ended romance.
Heart reconstituted: a brutally-ended love affair.
Love comes everyday but not clearly or softly;
its glitter shines on every cool girl's forehead.

How a Poem Is Like an Erection

The long and the short of it—
poetry is all about shift and slide.

Muses arrive and depart, or swoon in awe.
Control over outcomes, abysmal.
False flags seem like the norm.

A poem may have a classical form, although variations are tolerated,
   perhaps enjoyed.
Any poem may be a technology of mischief and delight
or have a starting rhythm rising into couplets.

> In poetry's spring, the pace is fabulous, incendiary, like grease
> through a goose;
> wild surprises, thick failures, twists and turns, soft excursions.
> Poems arrive easily then, or manifest in dreams at night.
> In the heat of summer, efforts meet diminishing juice.
> Occasionally a muse becomes captivating, makes incessant
> demands.
> In fall, poetry retreats to revision of past sights and sounds.
> In winter, flashbacks to exuberant successes commence.

Once spoken, where did the words go?

Pirate Mailbox

In Cincinnati, just south of the Hamilton County zoo, on a southeast corner where Erkenbrecher Avenue intersects Vine Street, stands a blue, street-side, totally official-looking pirate mailbox. It has been there for decades. Every five years, usually around 8:00 a.m. on a Monday morning, an undistinguished uniformed man gets out of an undistinguished but official-looking Ford van and comes over to roughly shake the mailbox for firmness, to touch up any scarred paint and to cover up any rust.

And, three times a week, year in-year out, an undistinguished blue-uniformed man, carrying a large leather bag on his shoulder and a set of keys on a long, brass keychain, walks down Vine Street to that corner and stops in front of the pirate mailbox. In no hurry, he kneels down, lifts his keys, selects one (about two inches long) and unlocks the broad side of the mailbox. Wearing light-blue latex gloves, working from the top of the heap inside on down, he carefully pulls handful after handful out and stuffs the stuff into his leather bag. Usually, he cleans the mailbox in about seven or eight minutes. After rechecking the inside from top to bottom, he straightens up, closes the access door, turns the lock-key opposite, removes it, then stands up and walks back down Vine with his swinging bag.

Daily, a waterfall of messages slips through that mailbox's hinged-top delivery slot. Hopes, taxes, legal notices or plaintiff's depositions, flyers, mailers, skin magazines, and so on. They are mostly never delivered; therefore, no waiting for any response. But occasionally the pirates, out of a sense of pity, after opening, reading, even annotating burning, lovestruck letters, may send them onward.

Occasionally, they replace a fetid lawyer's bond notes with a flowery letter, inscribed with hearts and flowers, and send it on too. They may rip out hot, smutty centerfolds and replace them with pet photo layouts. Occasionally, a gun clatters in through the top. More frequently, especially at night, needles. Even knives. Once or twice a month, a knotted plastic bag of dog poop.

Letters to god, to men, to girls, to older women. Every day welcomes new bales of love letters with weepings, joyfulness, banality, sex offers, worthlessness.

Neanderthal Love

The juice bar down at the corner.
That watering hole down in, like, Uganda—
gazelles rub shoulders with hot panthers.

The Iron Law of the Jungle prevails—
No aggression at the waterhole.
At least until prey reenter back-jungles.

The dive bar down at the corner.
The man at the bar hefts his elk femur,
twirls it twice, surveys the herd, picks
by looks—or brains—closes in nimbly.

A perfect doll, dolled up expectantly,
with small pet pterodactyl on long leash.

Divinity of Christ

Divinity of Christ:
The gathering light of candles scores
my guttering faith, a cyst—
refracted by these pithy flames

it needs endure a lance.
My frail faith, my Christocentric ill,
canst thou be ignorance,
or spite? Or *via negativa?*

Or, —no! Divinest sadism?
Were Christ at hand in living flesh
would He *His* grace and chrism
sustain—or bow to grace *this* man?

The search for truth sustains
the man—the quest for truth, a pathless
land. But truth bestained
sports tiny teeth—they know no end.

In truth, my faith has rived.
But He found His through life on earth;
now lifts His hand to shrive
my frail faith, to heal that wound.

Quite alien but curt:
neti neti! Not this, not this!
Such Upanishads avert
Christ's tender, holy blessing.

The Side the Light Is Coming From

Of all the moons rising high before dawn, for
some obscure reason the smallest ones brighten
first. Could it be those clement gods to whom

first light caters, like a drummer to angled mirrors?
All this seems to happen near shores lit
by enormous, anonymous seas of swirling brilliance.

That's how it always happens—you start to think
of any odd affair and, like the parable of each
distinguished student, a teacher soon arrives.

But light is never convinced until it finds a space
to fill; blackness is never a total shortage of light;
is something like writing without an alphabet.

These risings at dawn make art all too quite true,
but do not explain why love is so purple and cold.
Those muse-like gains—balance beams for soiled light;

these risen things—strengths for soft, ushering hands.
Wherever rich you seek, in strawlight may you find.

Snowman / R. J. Keeler

Miss Bonatred Looks across Her Fence

Miss Bonatred, precise about her fíxed fence,
indulges me my glance at angry, blackish ants.
She contemplates within her mind a sense
that she, distrait within her kitchen, has insignificance;

a sense that every bleakness, albeit incomplete,
has seared against her unsung soul. Elegiac,
she recalls the bristles of a Hudson's back seat
on her bare and aidless, once-young back.

As her fingers press her warm window's glass,
she reframes some pale winter dream
of pearls consumed along pink crevasses;
her mouth leaves runes on a vulgar plum.

Green use of me she'd like to have,
and enslavement in her finical cave.

That Eddyline

If he were like some old, busted-up kayak;
she like some other—she a little sleeker perhaps—
and at that moment
nothing but muddled, open water between them—
not much familiar to ward them.

Left alone, he had gone upstream; she,
meanwhile, meandered downstream
into hyperbolic interactions. Now,
only circularity and endemic loops between the two;
and some still water but only a tiny strip.

She and he sidling back and forth,
paralleling a not-too-high barrier; in time,
each may swim across into the other's aura.
But snappy fluid eddies can hurt and bruise,
throw parties into new whirlpools,
suck them down into bottom muck.

What else out on open water wants congruent regard?

A fast-moving, boy-meets-girl current slices through a faint barrier,
turns upward,
circles unintelligently onto itself; each partner walls off; both super-
harden; both eager to rejoin former distant flows, or join new petulant
streams, or travel out to subtle bounding turbulences.

All exquisitely plummy; two parties carefully navigate.
Could be dangerous,
could be advantageous, or not,
could be nothing at all,
or everything at once.

Or finding calm in fulsome currents of life.
The best way to do that: be aggressive when dealing
among corporal eddies.
Boy, make sure to lean upstream! Girl,
make sure to switch your cockpit lean to downstream
and paddle, hard as hell, out of down-welled

turbulent boils—a huge Charybdis within quieter coherent pools.

Deep, nearly parallel outcrops and mesoscales,
cloud-wide eddies of turbulence, arise. You both,
go practice your combat rolls.

Remembering Buddha

I sat down on the garden bench and steadied myself with my left hand. *That* left hand, the one with the ring finger. The ring finger, but no ring. And where was that ring, I wondered? Hmmm. I'd have to remember to look for it once I got back home. Well, got back to my apartment, which wasn't really quite *home* as I had come to know it during all those past years with him. I sat thinking of that moment, long ago.

Where's the ring, he asked?

Oh, I said, *I took it off this morning to do the dishes. It's on the windowsill over the sink.* I actually did think I left it there. He thought differently.

Go get it then, he said, a little flippantly. *Let's see it back on that pretty little finger.* For just a fraction of a second, I considered alternatives: Was he angry? Had I really left it there? Was he trying to start another fight? Had it fallen down the drain? *Sure, honey,* I said, as I walked across the floor toward the sunlit kitchen window.

I became aware, slowly, of the bench's cold wrought-iron frame; I pushed two left fingers through its twisted lattice and clenched my entire hand. The dull edges pinched the cleft between the fingers; I felt the seat's flat edges press my old, bony butt. I took a full breath, slowly let it out between my teeth, then returned to that day at the sink.

I stood still, looked out the window above the sink, out to our flower garden. I would not yet let myself look down to that windowsill. Not at least for another five seconds, the while I kept my eyes fixed on the garden statue of Happy Buddha outside. Then I breathed in once and let my eyes drop down to the sill.

Back there on the bench, I had thought, *How could I have been so careless? Next time, I'll need to bring along my shawl and gloves.* Although the sun in front of the bench was still out—low but centered on the far lake—the wrought iron did feel quite chilly. Now I thought about the cold there in the bench and the cold in my apartment and the hard, cold spot I had noticed yesterday, inside and just to the left of my stomach.

Requiem for John C. Holmes

A lanky, couldn't-be-more-ordinary guy from Ashville, Ohio;
had served his country honorably, even advocated for whales.

His personal trajectories were so much divided,
but thankfully not everyone is a robot;

we each have multiple edges and sad faces;
in others it's willingly called humanity

or at least perhaps called interesting. Holmes embodied
the sense that men and women were *not* all created equal.

How does he compare to a radio star's beautiful singing voice?
When you got right down to it, they're pretty much the same.

Morals? Do you need to ask or know? At end of day,
in each instance anatomy can be seen as destiny.

He may have been like an old tree trunk
rotting perpetually from inside out.

Not good-looking, really. An office boy he wasn't.

Diary of Transits

Late afternoon grass alive with light, with dutiful insects moving and
   no hesitations.
All day, sun haunts us, low and high, but today we are so tiny;
only one mountain rises higher and that one snugs the sky.

Only one passage back
to a world of feeling difficult and winding. Run
among as many stars as words, discard your shoes, run backwards.

I am the forest floor just above the music
that plays forever, unheard. Who angles
to dance among that complex life?

Stop hiding from those crows in that tall hopetail grass—
love has no meaning there,
there is only broken silence.

Three touches that most get to make:
   The first is flesh.
   The second is love.
   The third is family.

Snake Medicine

i. Snake medicine people—quite rare, like
dragonflies flittering aimlessly above Mercury's

blistering hostile plains; plains where every
left hand counts the tiny, light-pearly scales

on a papery, newly cast-off, found molt skin.

ii. When, all ectomorphic and very pliable,
we cache our purity to the rear, in false belief

we'll never, never repeat those twenty-three
horrendous dis-decorums of our last entangle-

ment. So frail, so fallible, so fragile, we need
just inhale firm, concentric love to comfort, to

surround us. What little modifies perigees,
year to serial year, apart cataclysm, torture?

iii. Only brute shamans like Hermes may
compare incomparables: say, *love,* against

thereafter-naked, cold snakes. So when
asked, he, Hermes, gestures elliptically

to the strangle of our twisted love relations.

iv. Black-skinned but harmless snake,
Godspeed; go enter some dark burrow

that befits your shedding dance. You pelt
along a path of feels, of smells, of musk;

and paths of ancient, guilty fear—deceptions
up an asinine, forbidden tree. So, cast off your

old-flame retardants, shift lovers, put the past
to past underneath upheaps of lies, sensible

cute transgressions, and petite cowardices.

v. A double-gold-banded snake slithers like
streaming-hot oil across a two-lane blacktop,

rippling off the right side at terminal velocity,
escapes through sun-burned side grass down

into cool, red-barked madrones.

What Ever Happened to Ursula Andress?
—Dr. No, 1963 film

Hard to contemplate
that the darling of
so many young men—
maybe young women also—
hot for her superstructure
and her softly appealing
docking fenders,
would, over this narrow time,
develop so many wrinkles,
sags, and brown spots

as to resemble, at end,
one of those very rare
Magdalenian conch
shells that she,
Honey Rider—tall,
preening in her
stunning white bikini,
her sharp diver's knife
outthrust, on Crab Key's
forbidden beach,
surprised—
was so keen to keep
out of 007's broad,
hungry hands.

Third Part: The Natural World

Snowman / R. J. Keeler

The Invention of the Snowman

This, the way it is: any attempt to contrive
or divide is fraught. Rugged justice.
Rules no help, nor books, planets, knives—

maybe a statesman like Augustus?
Know, a black crow can take a straight
wire, a bottle of worms, bend up

its farthest tip. That black crow eats
worms alive it's fished out, thinks
nothing of it. Or not. Whereas beliefs

maintain two hands, clumsy, left and right;
we set our clocks by this phenomenon.
It is late fall now, time for white.

Every strange epiphenomenon
has its own agenda or property
line. A known fact—snowmen are fallen,

lazy, shiftless, embody popery.
Zen master glances at his watch: *An hour
gone, all I accomplished—a mockery.*

An hour ahead, to which fault shall I bow?
An unfinished puzzle, despite three
pieces already here in hand. Avow

this darkest month; we need to learn to lean,
to reply. The question then becomes, *Why?*
The snowman does not move forward to intervene.

It has no will, no testament; it's a Beatrice
to heathen hells—an irrigorous edifice.

Cold Wind of the Night

Midnight. Yesterday it rained all day.
Wind from the south seems to not hurry,
patiently tossing across my face and hands,
delicately and softly brushing my hands.

Midnight. Push up on the wood window
frame, full open—no interpreters, since
the cold wind of the night speaks for itself
if it speaks at all. Best to state, it *carries* itself
to flood this heavy room, to blow crisp along walls.

Would we ever know, were this to be its last force
to sweep us out into far, cold undeservedness?
Shifting wind after rain seems to merit attention,
but to what? Midnight. The incoming
wind feels naïve and ever so delicate.

Thistles

I fill my back-bedroom's window bird feeder
over and over again during the cold winter days
with generous cups of thistle seeds and sunflower
seeds and cracked corn and millet and peanut.

The little brown-gray birds flock and fight
and push each other ruthlessly onto midair.
Why am I so surprised each year's spring
when my backyard erupts into jungle?

Snowman / R. J. Keeler

Regarding the Futility of Operating a Noisy Leaf Blower in Mid-November

The motions of a young man operating a noisy, gas-powered, leaf
blower on a graveled parking lot are
eternal and constant: left-to-right,
reversing quickly back
to right-to-left.

The distribution of dead leaves in an open space is called *ergodic*. Why
then, within a winter circle of slow-dying trees,
attempt a fall campaign to forestall; why
oppose such natural entropy? Trees
mark time through any long,
interrupted night, then
march right back into
winter tomorrow.

A recognized absurdity, well-known in winter circles—holding back an
oncoming tide of leaves; just like, in that single moment, clearing
browned leaves off some graveled parking lot while,
all around, tall, leaf-covered
trees lean in and
wait.

Nurse Log

And this day begins.

An old nurse log, half into
earth, still highly attuned.
A billion billion years to go;
this high-minded cycle never will end.

By almost noon, a private service rises
softly out of still-morning earth; gravity
becomes like a river, muddy and swift,
carrying inconsequential images
downhill. The eye of the needle
telescopes out, then back
to near-zero. Lahars arrive
out of nowhere to sweep
the old family dog back
into the broken bedroom closet.

The nurse log's aura is extreme at
scintillated purple, and warbles
as a silent echo.

Tomorrow morning
the sun rises solid black
but no one cares a lick.
Late in an unsunny afternoon
the man speaks; a book inside falls
spontaneously off a shelf,
opens to page 47. Reading
down the left side, 4th paragraph:
. . . *resurrection encircles the wounded beast.* . . .

Intricate mind-loops draw out quantum truths, illuminate the decaying
        nurse log's pandemics.
Mincing but confused, the well is dry, as is an organic, rotting mind.
If even one original thought arrived before the fall, it would surely be
        trampled and wetted.
How to fold the forest's mind like a wild animal around essences used
like burnt toast.

Ross Dam

The dirt-gravel path switches back from the parking lot off Route 20
down to the canyon's lip, and to first sight of Ross Dam and Ross Lake.

The lake itself winds eighteen miles north past the Canadian border,
fed by Silverhope Creek, an umbilical cord out of the North Cascades.

Like a blue ecliptic, the lake's choppy surface cuts the dam's face
a dozen feet below a walkway that spans the canyon's high eyebolts.

Begun by the Corps of Engineers in '43, completed by fathers and
uncles—their singular maleness infused far into that vast, convex face.

With hot concrete and curved steel rebar, those rough workers, cooks,
and surveyors shaped, in that raw ravine, more than just one tall paling.

The dam—rigid, curved up from its base; a swollen spinnaker
pressed out to straining by wind driven back up the dry canyon.

The mate—simpler. Its penetrable surface rippled blue-green and white
by gay, random breezes. But down its dark side, deep below and bluest,
tiny, wet crabs slide and pick at the dam's ochred foot.

At night, the lake strains and heaves against the rigid face.
The dam surrenders; arched, locked against the canyon.
In the morning, they are social again.

Without one thing to contain, a dam would just be a dry, non-Euclidean
tombstone. Without containment, a lake would be a sole ribbon of verse
down at some canyon's crease.

Daily, Ross Lake changes. Daily, another sparkling accessory
slips away through twirling, magnetic penstocks. After years,
all its water has gone downstream, down to Diablo Dam.

Flying the Hump

An arc, an arc of cold air, where pairs of untidy
animals sail up, by, then over highest peaks
of Andes or Nepal to yell out to gods or to speak,
then throw up their tusks or hooves to Aphrodite

or Zeus, happy in their freedom. Wind-streams
full of living hawks in pairs, and naked kestrels
in time and place, rise up in high, existential
layers of air. Tumbling pairs of flora, fauna, green

hummingbirds or algae, conchs in a stratosphere,
getting mixed around, exchanging parts and pieces.
New orders fully in costume emerge—hieroglyphics
that sight on stars by sextant and clock, nix fear.

Up there, a condor's wingspan is just a mote
hardly visible from land below without telescope.

Aloft, one can throw lightning bolts down—
down on evil exes, their pretenses, vortexes;
bounce hot bolts off any and all sordidness;
at so high up, air pockets are hard and mean.

Slides, swings, playrooms at hump's crest;
up there, life is good, maybe even great.
One gets perspective on their own fate,
can even look up at Milky Ways, at comets,

or count monarch butterflies streaming by.
Let us all reach out and down to arrange
fricatives, see vowels grow strong, strange
consonants drop out. Any ungoggled eye

gets wind-buffeted; up there, nothing goes wrong.
Rise up stars, no doubling back, no coasting down.

Signs

Broken, or tottering on the very edge,
or surprisingly dull, or ubiquitously bright,
signs consolidate paths to blight.
Sign's best signals can't always pledge

to importune the next town over—
their deep gulch's neon sign says, *Jump!*
Can we in fact believe it, though? Some
choose not to trust such broad passovers;

some may well make that leap of chance,
since their only apparent choice is—failure?
In any foreign state or mixed-up culture
Red usually signals, *Come, let's dance.*

So, you, back off, back away, trudge home;
garishness signals an intrusive undirective;
it presents to us troubles, or stirs up hives.
Ignore it, you end up in such gulch as loam.

Glossolalia

Consider the many sources of plenty:
roses, the mud-daubers in their nests,
the moon's night-rays that regulate
new-burgeoning grass.

What does it all speak to; what sermons raise a voice?
Who around here hears the news, garbled or bad?
Thin threads of stutterings or whispers
blare out into distances, onto exigencies.

Lizards twitch at dusk with divineness;
all of you here have nothing, nothing to say.
You may not hear the sounds of pain
bamboozled to the all-nines.

No turning back now, you've heard wonderful
words of Truth—go upscale as high as you can.

What's a Weed and What's a Flower?

While fall advances and victorious circles of
upturned flowers close up to rest for winter,

a wild, multicolor hummingbird in air must
pick its path: how far, where to go, to feed?

Dismayingly, it may not know; in mid-skitter-
ing flight, never cleanly decide what's a weed

or what's a honeyed flower. Neither do we.
It all depends. In one classic provincial lawn,

a weed's off-color; but, settled in a flowerpot
of finer porcelain, it reinvents to a loveliest

flower. So, some may, by judicious choice,
broaden their narrow tolerances—they can

appreciate, even encourage, what quantifies
as a tiny, unforeseen bump or dip in narrow,

trammeled roads. So everyone, everything,
has its safe harbor; so nothing is neglected,

cast aside, or grossly overlooked. Then, by
a clever botany, we learn that many weeds

presume to offer rarest, life-fixing remedies;
and the reverse—that a pretty, tame-looking

flower is perfectly hideous; in perfect secret
it may convey and hand us deadly poisons.

Who among our sitting lay, a priori, in truth,
says which is which—can resolve dichotomies?

Stone, She

Crush, she—
Crushed by blossoms;
As many as, well,
Since flowers appeared.

Fuse, she—
Fused since time,
Long past believing
And given to me.

Grind, she—
Ground like wheat,
By glaciers, forests,
As many as grain.

Press, she—
Pressed by breezes,
Soft, cold,
As married as air.

Stone, she.

Rewilding

Stand by the lip of a lone buzzing
prairie; sense, and sense again, a
scope—unqualified, large.
That is our given nature.

Go out, plant a wide circle of wildflowers
where exists no slim evidence of vigor.
Wild things, unlike you, are known, move slowly;
wild things are habits; like justice, grind exceedingly fine.

Calls for bearing, whispered, as clear as frost, may
bridle, everlastingly fail to widen your gaze. But
like lake waters following upon hidden moons,
all your interior spaces
make fantastic.

Begin inside, a little at a time.
But one must be careful. Look into every interstitial.
Like the veritable frog in the pot being pushed stage
left; like, mutatis mutandis,

Syrian war prisoners unsuspecting until the instant
they feel the noose around their necks,
here is the glue that cements the unsaid: Everything is connected,
everything changes.

Such words only carry us so far.
We have no word for it, then what do we call it?

How to Love a Plant

Simple—lift it, take it out into that close-by forest.
Walk in farther and farther, just like a young deer.
Look at every unmarked trail as if it were high beckoning.
Try not to justify; trudge, aimlessly or not.
Imagine many grass-lit clearings among ancient, ringed firs.
Each opening becomes an unknown space within wild greenness.
Wherever you pick will be safe and quiet, like a sparse grotto.
But soon you must prepare to part and to return.
Undertake at afternoon, while shadows move west to east.
Circle and circle; look carefully at all corners and angles.
Ask each tall tree, *Within this long lifetime, will you still be here*?
Certainly in coming seasons the grass will rise up, overtop.
That hand spade in your hip pocket—bring your left hand there.
Push the sharp spade tip deep; mark a broad, luminous circle.
Set your charge alive into that fresh, shaded burrow.
Say a blessing, even more than one.
Blessings may do no benefit but neither do they harm.
All this may take hours; you must reach home before sunset.
Back away now.

You may return in one year, but you may return only once.

Minimal Colors

Pink is the color of too much flour in pancakes. Also, for a touch of contrariness in a pool of seaweed.
Red, the color of fish kissing. Many, wrapped up in balls, gill into tail.
Silver, the color of a young witch forever denied knowledge, and beautiful. Or, is that *purple*?
So be it. *Black* is the color of Hammurabi's code; broken, then lost forever.
White, a swaying of the heart of Ivana's tree house, at forty times above leaning wind.
Lusp, the color on the face of sentinels left alone on edges of a forest.
Senkarbit, the color of betrayal of a man, by men.
Saltrake, of a woman, by a woman.

Black Swan

You, swan-god of Sacred Mountain,
   of clear
                    double-trilled waters;
   you may, within those firmly tucked
wings
   remain likened to a secret, white crystal.

You there, black one, you never knew,
    never cared; while all around you
   on calm, moon-dark lakes
      white swans paddled freely by.

Black swan, dark soul, on those quiet nights
              far inside your utter fourth quadrant, inside
   a wet, rayless swan-world, your base instinct
       is—*not certain?*—but the consequences, long-
singing.

Perhaps, all along, had we too folded
   too soon our new wings within those
              same invisible lines? Perhaps
     we all
   traveled along those same taut, pillared paths?

A mime-like swan paddles silently by and signals:
   Us don't particularly care about every usual facts.
   Instead us tribe conjure swanish mythic ways of
   life. Nods and cups both wings around.

Coming out of hidden bleakness
        and thus, seeing clearly now, you,
once a bespoke spiritual ship—inside as white
as may be seen—sense that *Everything Is Perfect*
     so pink roses will still open and close;
             an unintelligent
universe will still shiver or shrivel; then, it will all be
   never-ending light strewed hard, and crippling dusk.

   You might confess then about your nearly

Snowman / R. J. Keeler

                  vanished nightly kind, about your own pure,
innocently
       gathered whiteness, about whatever ever-darkness

     is around you.
                          Quietly, this coming spring
             will see you possibly for the first time—it will
happen
      and we will be surprised. Oh, to be quite white inside, not
even a green or blue; so definitive, so nonblack inside; not
like those lighted red and green and blue globes out
     in that lower garden full of happy evenings and dim nebulæ.

Birds

   Birds, likely sparkling blackbirds
swoop, turn, glide, apparently having such
great fun in almost imperceptible snow—
four wings over frozen grass. Far stage right
a woodpecker, or something, *raprapraps*
on a cold, centric oak or pine tree.

   I sit cross-legged just in front
of a stretch of brown-black, ice-buckled
earth. I sit here every morning, same time.
I breathe slowly, grasp at contemplation,
quietly desist and listen, cautiously dredge.

   Out in front of me, again those two
blackbirds squawk fiercely, contend for a tiny
white object; perhaps a bread crust? Out
beyond, early robins stalk, stalk, stalk, lunge
at Annelida—worms—or wood lice; swallow.

   How all this seems to work in apparent
simple concert? Do the same three simple laws
that govern shoaling flocks of starlings guide
everything? From where I sit, I hear seven
to nine birdsongs blend and intermingle.

   That almost imperceptible snow-
fall now seems to have started thickening.

Of Dark or Bright Forces

A Hero's journey wends from bright to dark
and usually, not always, back to bright.
No one wants to hear her truth recanted;
such as it was, it was outspoken and hot.

Air breaks way bright; cold force to gut.
What's this pensive honkey-tonk about?
Avalokiteśvara or Kali—
take your pick or send us a third.

Throw those golden ladders down to twilit
seas; there are no bottom-feeders there
below ocean's surface boundary. Dark?
Bright?—oh, give us pork and beans instead.

After this, every conceptual color
will need at least five legs—all whitish
like long candles in a darkened room.
Our Hero throws boxcars, dances off,

throws off socks and shoes, wiggles butt.
Goose that dark old bird; no mercy!
Hero says, *Can't see an end from here,
but heightened wildness is well in order.*

Not a Flower
—After a painting by Georgia O'Keefe

Not a painting of a flower.

A print of a photograph of a painting of a flower—
   a calendar page for August, with narrow white borders.
Larger than life, taken from the New Mexico desert.
Compelling. But the eye is pulled immediately across the purple petals
              to the center,
   dark like a tornado's funnel;
   and in its very core, two glowing dots of green fire
   like emeralds uncovered from some clump
   of volcanic Colombian mud.

Leaking around the edge of this flower are clouds of color.
Grey at the top, intense red-orange at the bottom left and the right, just
like the sky's
       wonderful color
   at sunset over New Mexico's highlands where she worked and died.

But this image is not symmetric; although there is some strange sense
              of symmetry:
   the main petals gather inward from the edge, push outward
   from the flat page, only to fall back
   down into a darkening center. Twelve
              opulent folds curve in
   like arms of some dark and glowing
   spiral nebulae.

The flower itself, as with lives,   is imperfect.
A few irregular dimples mark the upper petals.
And three or four notches mar the lower periphery;
   the red-orange sky bleeds through a large one
   on the lower left.

A field pulses between
       the fiery sky lying just outside the painting's edge
   and the glowing, mud-dark center —   purple-red
   on the most raised parts of the petals,
       but dark purple

Snowman / R. J. Keeler

for the falling back into the twelve spiral folds;
lighter blue and blue-purple on the right half
where, perhaps, light from the rising, new desert moon
    is reflected.

Every year, almost about this same time,
—in memoriam, M. N. and I. P.

tiny black ants—or maybe descendants—
arrive back indoors. For they invade
and strut around, take hostages, toss
everyone aside. They care not for
decorum. They care not for steeped-in
graciousness. They care not for light,
rising darkness, hot, cold, or time of
day. Ants' wants do not encompass
wild heroics; only seek tasty crumbs
dusted in palm oil, sugar, or saffron.

Only yesterday, lawless ant-scouts
formidably, efficiently mapped out
my grimy kitchen counter, ever-stuck
drawers, my ancient under-sink spills.
Not confused by connived decoys—salted
strategically to distract or disperse—
ants move to consolidate gains, hot
little phantomlike beachheads.

Then, before their welcome fades
away, before the fast-incoming fall,
ants formlessly slide down my counters
and bathroom walls, bushwhacking
back to basement hives, into fertile
welcoming soils. For they seem
quite small and painless.

Blest ant gods, please consummate
our numerous failings, especially for
stand-ins like bright, lost Michiko
and Isadora; please impose—for past
lapses we inflicted and you suffered—
on us your fairest punishments.

The Lead Mare

How this could all happen
needs to be fully examined;

lead mare always comes last
after geldings and two aunts.

She treads into deeper duff
mixed by four sets of hoofs.

Lead mare scents water out
ahead, whinnies a soft shout.

Lead mare nips a filly's flank;
early discipline quiets pranks

All horses swish horse flies.
All eyes happy; what, surprise?

Silly girl, that perky lead mare.
What the hell, she never cares!

Trust No One with Only One Oar

Sometime ago, even a long time, when everything almost stopped—perhaps though, just an instant *before* everything stopped; perhaps everything *did* stop for just an instant or two, but guess we'll never really know, we are not stopwatches or. . . . Well, the calendar turned over, college started; water dripped down slimy dormitory walls, fed the local fungus and the graduating moss. Strange; somehow the dripping never stopped or even went unnoticed. But dogma be dammed, catechistically better to think only about water—a focus. What does or does not lead to completion? Holes in all six pockets, so leak pennies or rare medallions; worms surface up top for their food. Without them, plants and animals sputter out, or start to limp uphill. I can't wait to get all my trace elements: craw-fill is just gorpy, is not spicy. Lobsters good source for cadmium, cobalt—aka their twisted motives and sisters. Hunt methodically for tubers, especially at earth's center. Strip off all outer-shell electrons, even the 6p valence ones. In a house or home, a living room transects vanadium to cobble together those most-famous cinnamon buns, but so narrowly. Console armatures wound too tight. Simpatico bartles. Seven-petaled leaves, man-eating plants. Dewy sunlight filters as if dirt, so go out, overwinter in the Sierra Madres. Them spectral waves, only a rare portion of gold, are necessitated for handsprings of earned life and not like. . . .

Twinned Sides

Trellises turned astern turn into latticeworks—
a *what's behind* confused with what's not,
a *what's ahead*. This time is not now your
time; instead, a nominal pause to recollect
a nuance or conversational thought or two;

opportunity, classically reflected, to solder
together so-free, temporal bazaars. Skies
gather to suggest exempla: Hestia, eldest
child—and youngest; feast wines let first—
and last; unmarried virgin—or home goddess?

Sidedness, baroque as dodo or sympathy:
thus, a simple post-and-slat fence adoringly
presents two sides—distinct; both duly
brown and discolored. But it divides yards
from all about—degrades a plot's symmetry.

Trellis, time, wine: one side's in—one's not.
One aims to show disfiguring, right-up posts.
The other—pleasingly hung right-to-left slats.
So, paint away those ugly outboard-facing posts,
give natives a smooth view of inner slats?

Don't Surrender to the Bear's Way

Not long ago you dreamt.
You, the son of the daughter
of the son of the god of heaven,
dreamt. Iceless, circumpolar,
left-handed, wary still of shadow,
you set down kinship with crushed ferns,
left off sucking paws for nourishment,
and, into what buckled topsoil, stood.

Warm tea of costmary leaves, a fig
pressed around mountain mint and slice
of Emmentaler, then cold stream water.
You breathed in, twice—smell of root cellar.
Your kitchen table sweated under last
autumn's magazines, wedding invitations,
refinancing gambles, and samples of type
"V" Eureka bags. Pretty soon you hit
bottom, set out to pay some bills. Why
have all the hours of this day gone?

rake

i read in a biography that a. einstein famously
asked profoundly simple questions. by chance,

would his question be like a clear, bright song?
would it arise straight from his most-open heart,

or arise only after long, thoughtful calculation?
would his dearest, young daughter listen and

understand, see immediately in her vivid mind
a rusting, discarded rake leaning far out to back,

its handle splotched black and brilliantly green
by raw, unimaginable, uncontrollable plant life?

On the Art of Sailing, Lost

Draft another sail, sail behind—let it pull us along:
a simple strategy; conserves time and manners, yet
consequential, else forevermore we'll trail behind.

Is surging out ahead much wiser? Do compasses'
readings render a shifting course of coarse wind
and tide? Losing a squirrely race is to lose a bet

cinched up at the starting gate: *Sure, we'll get across
the finish line still heads-up.* Raise old baby spectacles,
tilt those astigmatic surfaces amok, down, at cramped

concrete, bargain-basement bunkers full of blinking
colored lights, iridescent bulbs—and it's only July!
Which tactics to forge ahead, if capacious winds gust

or shift? Whether to jibe, heel, or run free? But, god, don't
unconsciously luff or lust for speed. A *real* constantness
begets hard resentments from action figures like Captain

America or Wonder Woman, so used to dramas. Your
choice: tide'll regularly come slack, will perforce return
twice-washed waters of bay, sound, inlet back to Mars.

One tiny ocean-borne figurine, white-sailed and -bowed,
splashing like an insignificant hanky amid vast waves
of spume and blue, might contemplate simpler tasks, e.g.—

shove mountains to Muhammad, alter distant skylines,
or blast deep passes where none were first present. Full
of topsails, gusts, heeling-overs, a dry, scooped-out pass

cuts canyons' floors into blasted rubble. *Hail*, carefree bees—
flickering intrafissure within shadows of drier, fulsome
sunlight. But what are newly crated spinnakers for—for

good use or just to ornament a hull? Or just to block
views out ahead, or lift a watered prow to skim across
a swell? No, *do* hoist up that cellophane-like dragonfly

wing. Best to drive a two-masted sloop down heavily
to its end course, to complete its run, than to give a jib
or mainsail rest; *don't* permit them rest. Everyone, blue-

water sailor or mariner or captain, needs a manifesto
to help set their course. Here is one—try it on: pluck
out tiny, annoying slivers of elm mastwood from

swollen fingers; well, but do not seek to punish *all*
sliver-birthing trees; do not encover them in tangled,
evil-killing vines. Anyway, it's done now; punishing

those waterwoods would be ingloriously ineffective.
Wounds heal over a natural arc of time; tiny sliver-
scars turn to remnant hardness, good for tight-hauling

in mainstays; any lack of nerve sense becomes an aside,
interesting but irrepresentational—it's all a cover, even lie,
about reverse-flying, bleached-linen genoas, all fancy things.

Suppose the Rainy Season

        i.
If in Amazonia my grasping hand incites
a buzzing bee, will those recurring
feelings inscribe some dainty portraiture?
If so, my ragged soul begs off the firmament.

        ii.
I go about my garden, I trim and straighten,
brighten; the while a covert snail inches slow
into sun. So then my sprinkling may glisten
his slipperiness of travel, just as rain slicks
my own evening's sacramental walk.

        iii.
An armature of poignant flowers invites a new-
skinned monarch to tack across a just-mowed
lawn; at morning, a ruddy bug makes assault
on bulbs that limp to light through crusty larch.

        iv.
Vapors drift away off piled-high thunderheads;
like principalities of consciousness, they condense.
Beneath them, we finger-paint our thoughts—so
messy they can be, but brilliant; while at side,
our tinny cleaning cans slink toward inky gray.

        v.
Those wild ocelots of thought propose, *Deny
my frosty little penances?* So, I scatter winks to
doubters that offset, even counter, their azured
gravities. *Evenings glide to dark, swallows off to flit.*

        vi.
I'm like one who senses all frequencies a sinner's
heart may measure—a harmony of sound or sense.
Might some gift restore my inner peace? Or might a
child's compass, aloof in child's hands, swing around
the wintery earth below it, by force of ferrous needle?

Cold Rain

Pelts dying grass and brownish, fallen leaves.
Expert rain jujitsus down to worm lairs,
bullies them; fastens doorknobs upon exiting
upstream so as not to leave worms to drown.

Cold rain confesses all sins, buys absolution
over tribes of nematodes—soak a wafer, shun
the wine. Moisture can't unstick nor lubricate
stuck tongues where false emotions can't relate.

Cold rain professes kindness; however much
it lies, it needlessly tells consequential truths.
Rain cycles up to hated sky, to thundercloud;
conscripts warmth of mists too soon devout.

Cold pelting rain cannot tell time; topples
gigantic ferns and larches, stacks colossal
mounds of detritus up, which serve to funnel
moistness underearth, down naked tunnels.

Cold rain condenses steaming worlds into one.

Four and a Half Haiku for Spring

Silly old rhizome
Please don't be so shy this year
Ripping hot cartwheels

Green leaf brown leaf dance
Buck up flowers give stink eye
Ripe scent of quelled pear

Cold electric rain
Worms scurry to don rubbers
Hummingbird stops in

Haughty trimmed bonsai
Cut snip cut snip contemplate
Yikes time to pay rent

Wild beasts maneuver
Caterpillars waltz down stump

Snowman / R. J. Keeler

Fourth Part:
Science, Fun, Odds & Ends

Snowman / R. J. Keeler

Oh, Make-Believe

Copper is gold and gold is cotton and cotton is mud.
Say it faster, spin to the left, and pinch your cheek.
> *There once was a turtle that slept in a cloud—*
> *an Icelandic programmer, one hell of a geek.*

Please Lord, forgive, she transected the Talmud
into counterexample, metafiction, and leek.
> *They went down the bunny trail, hand in hand—*
> *Bach to division, Escher to float, and Gödel to pink.*

Sit with numb butt—leap, lance that koan! Beginner's mind
faints, bows, bows again, then pukes in the sink.
> *Hippety-hop, hippety-hop, garage sales propound*
> *our Universal Undecadent Law—Conservation of Junk.*

Epitaph for Pre-consent Decree AT&T

> b. March 3, 1885
> d. (dismembered) August 24, 1982
> Size didn't matter

Lean, mean, Judge Greene:
Time to fold, elephantine.

The hairy man from the bottom
   of the lake strings microwave towers
   between Chicago and St. Louis.

You, AT&T, try to drain this lake,
   throwing up peevish regulation.
   But widows and orphans turn against you.

        Lean, mean, Judge Greene:
        Too fat, too slow, you have to go.

Patrician, well-drilled, too *cher*
   with Justice to convulse,
   Systems Engineering so mainstay;

you, AT&T, alchemized *Holy Roman Empire*
   into *Modified Final Judgment*.
   Done in by, oh, such unimagined ecology.

The Twice-Born

The photographer
at the farthest edge of the crowd
records for authorities
all the craziness and inanity
of the gathered populace.
Much later, he will be rewarded.

The photographer is a voyeur.
Better they than I, he thinks,
as he brushes dust off his
wide-angle lens.
Every spring, he returns to this
same village square to film.

On two separate nights, on visits
to document wild crowds,
the voyeur saw and twice captured
on different films a distinct face
he thought—no, was very sure—he knew.

After developing and pinning up
those separate films—still dripping fixer—
on each of two nights, he scoured
the fresh, clear negatives to locate
the distinct face he was sure he knew.

But, against each negative's coal-black background,
the voyeur had only comprehended
on each one
a marked, tight image—
an image of a small, white, floating bird.

Tomorrow, this year's photography
done, he will plan a long vacation.
He is thinking
about the Seychelles.
He will carry
his large, fixed-format camera.
Should he invite his friend Edie?

Of What Use Is a Bungee Cord in a Clever Universe Full of Time?

Open James Walker's college physics
text, 2nd edition; page to Ch. 8, read
there an annotated e-diagram of previous
attempts to correct a persistent problem.
Included is a list of parts and optional
spares required to disassemble and
reconstruct a universe; even a hot-
linked list of tools for this task, modified
through many earlier attempts.

Careful not to drop a tiny screw or
hex-nut—an entire swath of galaxies
giga-light-years across might evaporate
or suddenly collide. And please,
for that repair job use plenty of light
such as a hand-held Costco tactical
flashlight. By the way, also recall,
according to Brian Greene, or was it
Stephen Hawking, the concept known
as "light" is almost always a convenient
scientific synonym for "time."

And recall that in other tawdry
side-rooms where the natural
topology of homeomorphisms
is fleshed out, "time" is also
synonymous with the concept
of "knotting," as in "knotting of time"—
not, alas, synonymous with "knotting"
that unfolds in discrete bedrooms
of BDSMers—and a bungee cord
hanging off an extravagantly long title
is capable, potentially, of a knot.

Interesting that the same cord may,
in the right hands, be a perfectly
handy implement to employ to tame
a known, unruly universe—which,

by the way, may not be an *entire* universe
due to established and rigorously proven
constraints on the maximum propagation
speed of light—and to contain all its variant
excesses and wild excursions.

Since the universe is a well-known, clever
trickster—so titled—its wild excesses
may have their downsides, their petite disasters,
usually in a form of dangerously inflated
thinking, or else plain, crude selfishness
or thoughtlessness with regard to another's
sensitivities or trajectories.

So that tiny screw somewhere down there
on a carpet, the one you dropped just
four stanzas back—turns out it's the key
to attaching a bungee cord's end-hook
to a sharp prominence like the south-most
spiky tip of Ursa Major's far-redshifted
galaxy GN-z11.

There—once it's been hooked, swiftly run
the cord back under and around
the universe's belly (to some astrophysical
grammarians it's plural: "universes' belly"
or "…bellies") thereby preventing
an alleged, and now seen as the really
thoughtless, infinite, and never-ending
expansion which Alan Guth, in 1979,
at age 32, while teaching up at Cornell,
theoretically predicted.

Then, once the clever universe's never-
ending expansion has been limited
and stopped by the non-infinite (or
non-Guthian) expansionary limitations
of that particularly finite bungee cord
(also known in Australia as kangaroo,
octopus, or "occy" straps), everyone
can rest easy again.

Snowman / R. J. Keeler

BTW, a bungee cord's core comprises several
very-elastic, interwoven rubber strands; its sheath,
woven out of common cotton or polypropylene
and typically braided with its inelastic
threads spiraling around these inner rubber
strands, will *not* materially expand. Thus,

any sustained longitudinal pull on a cord—say,
by the cosmological constant Λ, lambda,
monotonically increasing over normal, infinite
time—will cause the outer polypropylene
sheathing to neck down, squeeze, and
quickly constrain the inner rubber
strands. A convenient calculation given
in that same 2nd edition physics textbook
proves that compressing a sheath
in this manner quickly translates into
longitudinal stabilization of an entire
bungee cord.

Rigged thusly, the outward push of Guth's
inflationary universe just equals the inward
pull of a hooked, stretched bungee cord,
so universal symmetrical stasis obtains,
finally.

But there may ensue some quite-lengthy
oscillations while those two opposing
forces negotiate a balanced truce: each
oscillation may shed a tiny quantum
of mass-energy out into spacetime
or maybe back inside—who except
Hawking would really know. Most
oscillations dampen out; over time
perturbations lessen; given much
more time, everything stops moving;

unless someone unclever—or clever,
depending on your attitude towards fun
and boisterousness—cuts the bungee cord
in two, severing it cleanly north of Pleiades.
Then all bets are off, since the locomotive

snap-back of a severed bungee cord
may be just powerful enough to dissect
a known-unknown universe into two
fairly equal but raw halves.

(Please do note that bungees are a major
source of eye injury, so medical doctors
suggest not using them carelessly—unless
of course a universe is headed, as
described herein, for melt-down.)

But after that snap-back, each new half-universe
would again be unconstrained; unfortunately,
just as before, both raw halves would return to
Guth's never-ending 1979 expansion protocol.

Nota bene: before that schism happens, be
very sure you plan to end up in the right
half, not the wrong half. For example, you'd
want your dog and cat and Platinum Amex
card in the one you were in, but all your
ex-wives and ex-bosses and scientific
competitors in another half.

So then someone, neither Guth nor Hawking,
must now go buy two more bungee cords
and hire a second pair of hands to re-constrain
both those expanding half-universes. Should
that scenario continue *ad nauseam,* one
may observe the writing on a wall: more
bungee cords numbering to an expanding
power of two and the same in pairs-of-hands,
to achieve each re-fastening after each schism.

Hence Zeno's familiar paradox's quirkiness:
the so-clever universe *does* get the last laugh
since Mr. Big Enchilada here just keeps getting
cut in half every cycle, while the demand for
more and more cords escalates by a power
of two. Go do the math:

any stock of bungee cords is more-or-less finite,

at least in local Ace Hardware stores, so an
inventory runs out well before the universe
becomes un-Dumpty-like unbroken and re-glued.

Of course, there's another reasonably likely scenario:
behind everybody's back an ever-halving universe,
clever to a fault per the title, is frantically glomping
back together those ever-calving micro-universes as if
they were tiny balls of mercury, element Hg, skittering
around on some flat Qing Dynasty porcelain plate.

Consequently, again per poor old Zeno, if this were
a celestial Broadway musical there may never be *any*
end note nor finale before a never-last movement
of a not-last sonata; so once again the clever universe
would win by default.

In any case, bare, now-unknotted time keeps on going—
not chunked-up or minced-up—so then perhaps way out
there in far barn-red Zeta-land, it is steady boring *time*
that actually wins and not Mr. Big Enchilada. Stay tuned.

And "time"—no one cares about boring time;
time's only the faintest melody underneath what
for some time now has seemed like a vast, unruly,
and perhaps *a cappella* score.

Moon's Muscle Memory
>*Archeological Inventory at Tranquility Base*
>—The Lunar Legacy Project

It was the lightest, simplest of touch, but
it burned. Exquisite of course.
And captivating.

Out here, at Tranquility Base, only loneliness now.
But,
doesn't moon water have muscle memory? It can't
be too hard to prove.

Appears there's nothing at Tranquility Base to stop raw desire,
it'll just flower up again like any arm does, or some palm
in some cases might—water just claims its own presence.

Any sensitive touch may be felt for a brief moment, a briefest;
perhaps one should be careful where, when, they reach out.

Skin isn't like raw moondust, not incredibly soft nor inviting regret.
Skin leaves its own wake in water if touched or unwrapped.

And gravity has no sense nor memory, might blindly throw out touches.
Memory is fallible, we know—serves up ever-present happiness,
    ditches the rest.
Memory's umbra and penumbra cannot replace now-soft hands or
    wanting skin.

Advancing shadows are recollection of sin—to never touch or ever be
    close.
At end, memory can do anything, even recirculate itself, even rekindle
    itself.
At end, memory knows zero of itself; it searches for warmth in any
    distant arms.

At Base, now that everyone's gone home—desolation, except for one
gnomon; lost, buried in moondust's fabric.

Full stop about forthcoming tenderness, especially any human variety.

Snowman / R. J. Keeler

What happens when all longshots play out, in touch or mostly empty water?
Either flow breaks wide open, or moon water comes to a sudden halt.

Training Your Intuition

There is instinct, and then there is intuition.
The human psyche—vastly complex but simple;
once it breaks, where to be after its departure?

Observe an oncoming train of white-stippled,
far-out waves and guess which one will skin
or crush you first? Should one flee on instinct

but smile against somewhat fainter intuition?
Look here—pick elevator *cinque*,
place your bet as though we're playing a game.

When *due* unloads a startled fleet of Andalusian
horses, were we right or wrong or—even vain?
But misapprehend your fertile girlfriend's

period—did intuition turn on itself
or, maybe, did instinct finally win?

Head End Hop Off

Critically lacking in judgment,
                              that ur-conscious nature
                              foreclosed loopholes forever
    by looping intelli-strings around my heart.
      Some tightly, some more loose,
but all steeped and sorted, full
of invictus
    and a paler vinegar.

                Instantly, a cache
of hoarded, un-interrupted signals leapt across a pure
silicon gap into a pure receiving
    tray, then scooted off into the faint,
    dark eclipses of yellow sun-limbs:
  gaseous, billowing, frozen in time,
        hopeful but still, secondarily filed

                      under *Do Not Disturb*. Spell it
    out in all-caps, filter it through a #4
    unbleached paper cone—no spills.
              Their soft pubic regions throb with
              insouciancent red bile; they wear
the hot corrective lens of a final
trunk-line switch. Point-to-point, anyone?

The Sound of Rushing Water

Emmanuel came home one day to find his goats were loose.
Someone was supposed to watch them
but got drunk.

The goats went to the beach to surf and tan.
Four-footed surfboards in short supply.
Suntan lotion hard to work in through the fur.

Slippery river rocks;
fish pools in cold water;
small rainbows over the shallow falls.

How We Learn

Were you disappointed, lovey? Did you expect something more? No. Did you think it would be better? It was long, Wendy. . . . It took a long time. Yes. And then it was sudden. . . . Of course, darling.
—J. Kozol, *The Fume of Poppies*

Here—
go inside. Stand to front of any multipaned window—
large, singular, dimensional. Look

as a fantastic signal, like intense light, streaks
nascent glass. That signal will
comprehensively engulf you—befriend
you with its feel of dire knowings.

We start our transit as avid learners; exercise profitable
desires against fabulous windows.
But haste to learn, to grasp, incurs
roundabouting—painstaking and contrary—
which encircles one's stagnant, bound flesh

anchored in material diva-ships, naïve postures.
Instead, surrender to oncoming vibrancy,
or exotic lightness.

Though we—exceptionally eager pupils—
may *not* grasp anything of note, never
attempt to install our reliquary-like, material selves
into position or pose, to gather raw

transmuted elegances; weakened efforts
to advance our sly tardiness or spell
our history, or—always aforemast—
relegate us back into passivity.

At end, we do not so much learn
as bodily selves. We give over
to transacting powers that infiltrate
our insubstantial frames and, next,
teach us softly.

Ode to the Syrian Arab Republic on Our Tax Day, April 17, 2018

Desert swallows everything;
symphonies erupt overnight.
Not everything could be right.
The hell, go replace our king.

Quartz swallows sallow lady;
oasis's waters burble, burble.
Perovskite sands blind Virgil;
what to do, poet—a ruba'i?

Loch Ness serpent graduates;
another attorney? No, a nurse.
Posies and snapdragons avert
her bad day; flowers animate.

Stravinsky, Debussy, or Liszt?
Strut those symphonies, G clef.
Jazz, polyrhythms for our deaf;
ragtime sears our justly kissed.

National security or old pizza?
Missiles skimming desert sand;
pepperoni, tomato, garlic, ham.
Turn it all over to Mother Teresa.

Pluto Haiku

Pluto hangs in south
winter sky. Or does it? Killed
off by IAU.

Dark Abstraction
          —after *Dark Abstraction* by Georgia O'Keeffe, 1924

i.
The blue is pushing into the red; that's simple.

Mind begs to see it differently: some objective thing here and
alongside, some other abstract thing

which could be spun out considerably—this painting, abstract; an
abridgement, summary, containing substance; not concrete, not reality;
something external, independent of mind.

Still, the blue is pushing into the red.

ii.
Has actually pushed red nearly off-canvas. A serpent-shaped,
milky ribbon between them is. . . .

The painter explains, *A hill or a tree cannot make a good painting just
because it is a hill or a tree. . . . Abstraction is often the most definite
form for the intangible thing. . . .*

Two, maybe three, organic forms set against each other.

In this 1924 painting, an organic form of blue sets against a red form.

Inside each red and blue form, on the edge, are darkened oblique
structures
that can be thought of as some internal transformation of each other's
colors—a response to some disjunction

we can only guess at.

In this painting, blue, on the spectator's left, is floating into red
on the right. The organic form of blue sets against similar red

iii.
in the realit.y

There, .

Snowman / R. J. Keeler

Whereas : an.

I will concentrate on the salience of white in this abstraction
and attempt to conclude, perhaps, something Biblical. First,
in a few words . . . .

promotes this abstraction.

Four basic colors, but saying white is a color,
made this abstraction. Miss O'Keeffe. . . .

iv.
A thing cannot make good art just because it is;
[do not] separate objective from abstract;
the abstraction is often the most definite form for [the] intangible.

Blue is winning and has pushed red   off-center right.
Closed, cool is winning and has pushed emotion off-center right.

Mind is winning and has pushed emotion right.

Lava flows up between the two

v.
Milk of heaven flows down between the two.
Black has split off from red at the base and is integrating into blue.
Black is separating into blue and red.

Adam [blue], Eve [red].
The ___ snakes up the middle.
Adam is in blue trunks and has Eve [here today in red] on the ropes.
             god'S THE PROMOTER. tHE SNAKE'S THE REF.
Adam's dark part is belly-to-belly with hers, but hers is splitting
       and retreating.

From the lower right corner, a light illuminates the scene; at the top,
light [the snake] breaks through blue and decapitates him.

vi.
Part of him is floating over onto her.

The blue is pushing into the red; that's simple.

Spirit Level

I. Build
Our scruffy apprentice mason,
first name Byron, stomps a longish line
of terrain, thus leveling and packing soft,
fallen, black stardust, firmed to a plinth
by his size-13. Byron flips his spent Camel
Turkish Gold at passerines
out ahead—one jackdaw
prances southward, offended. Byron's
mason steps in to lay down his antique,
hued, triple-bubble spirit level;
stands to watch clear liquid droplets
re-align. Grunts, nods. Apprentice
spoons a half-quart glob of dullish
mortar on the base plinth;
squats to grab two chance bricks
off an upturned, jumbled pile;
gracelessly lofts each to his master.
One, two red clay bricks—inert, unliquid—
descend via hard, skilled hands
down into mortar.

II. Reverence
A station—like a long fleck of white-gold-
black-gray foam—spins aloft upon a girdle,
a sou-earthly cage, some eighty leagues high.
Dika, a girl almost twenty-nine, of Romani
lineage, drifts outside; she lays rearward, prone
to a blue ball of water. Were she now so moved—
black-speckled dome above, blue oceans
underneath—to permit a moist sacrament,
her teardrop would float
within her gold-patina helmet, just under
blondish lashes. Her faint, shadowy, yang
animus piggybacks; it glides in parallel with her—
and so—katsu! Dutifully, her animus
and tear are falling and catching,
endlessly falling and catching.

III. Curiosity
From far, far outboard
the Horsehead Nebula—countless parsecs
hence—some jumbled, ghostly, spiders' cords
swipe at, nudge and then cradle—
both that distant, still-prone Romani
girl; a dismal, bluish snowball-comet,
starlight-burnished; Byron's left
size-13 boot; and a third brick tossed
to the master bricklayer—all falling,
falling, falling in or toward their
unique, disparate hive. Then, just
at local Louisiana sunrise and instantly
in Hanford, a pair of tuned-LIGO-mirrors
tickle, skitter, gently throb,
then quietly re-align.

Doxology
—United States Navy, *The Navy Hymn*

Eternal Father, strong to save,

The sermon commences. Ol' Apollyon, the Angel of the Bottomless Pit, wakes, shakes off the current hangover. Fumbles on the bed-stand for the pastel crayons, must get that dream down onto paper. It was so weird: dirigibles dive-bombing a scum-locked lake above the Los Alamos Dam, dropping broiled cheeseburgers inside half-buns. Where the fucks were his spectacles?

Whose arm hath bound the restless wave,

Sayonara, buster! The Founder of Murder gets his plump duff off the couch to go toss his mid-term ballot into the library drop-box. Too bad. . . . Sure wish Ross Perot had run again; maybe 86 *is* a bit too old? Golly could he, should he, renew his membership at the downtown health club?

Who bidd'st the mighty ocean deep. . .

Right—the ocean deep. Have to go look into that, soon. Lusitania, Thresher, Princess Amelia, Spanish Armada , etc., etc. Took them all down, ha ha. Just clean the toilet bowl every day, use Ajax or such. Better than spit. Who's out there sailing right now? Feckless mariners! I particularly favor those below-decks engineers.

Its own appointed limits keep;

Crap! My SSA payment only goes up 2% next year. Have to find some other way to get smack. Goose them archangels down there to empty more pockets from the fallen—even the un-fallen, if they hove too close to my heat. Put on my dark welder's goggles, go below and check up on my tallies.

Oh, hear us when we cry to Thee. . .

Cry to Thee? Too late for that, buddy. Should have done that before the Big Change! Thought you could get away with all that messing around, scalping high-school basketball tix, stepping on sidewalk bugs, shorting the IRS? We have eyes and ears everywhere, sorry. Gave lessons to GCHQ.

For those in peril on the sea!

Yeah yeah yeah. Go jump in a lake. Pray your Pater Nosters or misbahah or love beads. So go sue me! I hate yellow flowers. Also red. I heard yesterday that some say, *I'm the real reason that male sperm counts are falling all across the western world.* I need to have someone build up more raised flower beds for me.

Protect them by thy guarding hand...
Protect them whereso'er they go...
From rock and tempest, fire and foe. ...

22 Reasons Why There Is Such Widespread Emphasis on Zombies These Days

1. Transfusions are all the rage for building and solidifying relationships.
2. The entering Harvard class of 2020 is 32.3% zombies.
3. Zombies are such reliable workers; they never ask for overtime.
4. Zombies are such reliable workers; they can even work in service industries.
5. Contrary to fact, zombies make good, gentle, day-care workers.
6. Turn a zombie inside out, they sparkle.
7. Zombies don't ever fart in bed.
8. Knock Knock. Who's there? A zombie with lemonade.
9. (Zombie jokes make no sense to nonzombies.)
10. Zombie dogs rule, zombie cats drool.
11. Why couldn't a Norwegian zombie in the 1944 Olympics clear the high jump?
12. Answer: Heavy water. But also see #9.
13. In 1896, a zombie came in second for the Nobel Prize in medicine and physiology.
14. Zombies become quite nice if you tickle them for ten minutes.
15. Zombies never claim term life insurance deductions on their state or federal income taxes.
16. Zombies vacation in eastern Haiti.
17. Zombies have to drink up to sixteen energy drinks a day to be reanimated.
18. Bela Lugosi was a closet zombie.
19. A flambéed zombie always makes for a better chef.
20. We are still waiting for that zombie apocalypse.
21. The Z Nation is currently situated in lower Bosnia and Herzegovina.
22. Zombie poets are not called *writers*, they're called *content providers*.

Regarding a Recent Call from Heather in Account Services

Considering my account's near zip, and late,
I suppose Heather had warrant to call today.
But immediately I hung up on her tender

voice. Then a huge dirigible, a Hinden-
burg, nosed itself directly into Heather's
soft-wall Iowa cubicle, to lay its head

onto her lap. *Come with me, Heather; depart*
this barrenness, sell those old muni bonds;
move back to Brooklyn, lease some squalid studio,

become a derelict painter. Or, go hammer
your little toe! So yesterday, I mailed a box
of fifteen ripe cantaloupes to Account

Services, in lieu of all my bad checks.
Heather, I promise, next time I
will take your call.

A Long Residential Sadness

Invisibility's lack illumined his low sin—so cheesy!
Not possible to now turn back, to recall a word
that, like Việt Nam's napalm jelly, sent third-degree
burns onto the entire corpus of his deftless work,

withering spaces, paragraphs, plots—even carets.
All colors of his brightest rainbow, including
its noncolors, can't ever smudge out or redirect.
Tentacles of offenses against language deluded

untold professors, proofreaders, and bookbinders;
they wouldn't see the truth, urged *Benefit of Doubt!*
He tried to cover his misstrike by deft or dimers,
take-backs. He burned texts, mouthed, *Not my fault!*

But a jury of peers' opinion was that, published or not,
'twas foul—no one claims to hit *f* when he meant *d*uck.

Snowman / R. J. Keeler

Last Part: Literature

Snowman / R. J. Keeler

Snowman / R. J. Keeler

Meaning Has No Matter outside of Sound
—after "The Emperor of Ice-Cream," by Wallace Stevens

Strike out sequential consonants,
Waste lorn fricatives, and permit them swage
Any remainders through rusted radiators.
Let heroics meld in solemn somnambulance
As cause for epitaphs written in Esperanto
And pegged to next year's purposeless sins.
Let metadiscourse and disfluencies abound.
Meaning has no matter outside of sound.

Lay onto the parchment of peaches,
Dense by arrhythmic inclines, those words
Troubling for ears in refuse to connect,
And conspire them to mock epics of size.
If their pseudonyms obtrude, the better
To hide warrior from clown, and forbear.
Let the autotelic message dumbfound.
Meaning has no matter outside of sound.

W
—UVWX

You are fat and probably a bastard.

That dexterous character alongside—a double-crosser if ever I saw one.
Archetypal sex maniac—he, legs splayed indelicately, the casual taunt.
(Naturally, I try not to glance directly at his journeyman's plexus.)

So . . . help me out here. Why the family with your surname resides so
    far apart?
Two entire blocks to the left. Not hiding anything there? Of course not.

But. A matter of record *not* requiring stipulation—your sinister
    neighbor, the vixen?
Remarkable, the sharply chiseled resemblance.

Oh, you semigod, the only double-wide in the pack—go diet!

Calling Something by a Different Name

Too often I fail to see my motives, thus
soon fail again. A wet, bicolor parrot fish
writhes and pants on deck. I crush its skull.
Remorse, reflection? No, none, not a whit.

Again, I soon re-debase, deflower: ground doves,
horned beetles, hairless snakes—never to flourish.
Apart Metta, against Precepts, my dull
will wins. So, then, remit—*reverse names' façades*.

Thus, dolphins' names—not *Dolphin*—are inbred,
matchless, self-whistles. Thus, apotropaic
names *do* deflect demons—and ugly ones mislead!
For Philip—Greek, *Philippos*—*horse-lover* is mimic.

Thus, an exorcist, one hears, can't expel a demon
until the demon is forced to surrender its name.

Base Flow, Drought Flow

Whom to distract—from wetness relevant
to moist, to flow, to less quiet essences?
A hot African rift bends into sharp eastern
earth creases; two speckled antelope

swerve astride at fallen gravel, whiff
bared-up sandstone. Two paws, remarked
by hooves, turn tan sand jelly-like,
mix up past year's moist base flows.

So, we trek beyond the barn, uncap a well
that's augered deeper every season not wet.
Bring gourds, old barrels, tubs to carry water.
But water doesn't last—sun offsets showers.

Circulate imagination or it will dry up.
Suppose that's to be expected; so stop
your mental resurrections, mental seeps;
be like foxes come to lap wet pebbles.

Our formless liquid lubricant in winter
is hard, not wet; its transubstantiation
signals a bent to run to higher ground.
Your flagging manuscripts—shelve or burn?

What dries them up? Dryness. Work must be
quick and final. Our arterial blood
floods through hot imaginings or else bleeds
an art's vital fluid—we all piss inky black.

This covert flow—for antelope so crucial,
for us, a lifeblood's task we'll not regret.
Not ever painted into corners, so percolates
way deep—we pain to feel our tiny glaciers.

Kicked to the Curb

I.   Could be anything   like Shakespeare over easy,

like a kick to the curb   like cracks to papier-mâchéd time,
or a little thing   misunderstood between us;
something as simple   as a severe botch
like when we both caught   that simian influenza.
Awkward wasn't it, though;   you could have made it
if you hadn't stopped
if you hadn't kissed   me   so deeply after that chilly swim.
Felt like it was an anteater's tongue   inside me.
My god what else can   you do with that thing?

II.   If only I hadn't

cut up her credit
cards or filched
her mail, canceled
Yahoo, she might
have heard
the news, recanted,
folded, been blown
to the curb like
a stinkbug high on
raw Febreze fumes.

III.   A flip cat warily covered in gold glitter then kicked to a curb;

you may now see her in all-dark snow, but so can rats, so any mutt.
But, as their own top dog is way bygone, ha, curbed too, then fourteen
long up-tailed Fuji id magicians make wills, gift us wandx collections.

Prey Drive as Metaphor

> "Tho' Nature, red in tooth and claw. . . ."
> —Alfred, Lord Tennyson, "In Memoriam A. H. H."

Start with a torrid complex, a twofold affair;
herd prey onto lignite flatness (somewhere open),
then consecrate. Start searching—right there.
Learn topography, study runes, select potent

colors, words, or dances. Stalk wily, dazzling
apparati as if old gazelles; invoke cool, cunning
tropology; craft conceits, pen pseudograsslands.
Go expand a canvas, spike stagecraft—nothing

unchased. Soon, a poem tendered, a stage swept.
Wait adroitly. Congeal verbs and pigments; sore
ligaments ministered. *Once bitten, twice shy* leaps
to mind, but disregard. Old masters decline afore.

Prey drive a dualistic inclination, most inevitable.
Posited of all wolves—or of Rodin, Satie, Hubble.

See What Happens

It would really be something to visit inside
our sun to see what presently occurs;
still later, get to have a cold cherry popsicle.

But this time must be different, much different.
See what happens when you go with the flow?

So our girl hesitates, but then launches herself
into consequences; her views go click-click. Every-
one else becomes a lemming, rushes to a far edge

and jumps off. Ok, there—go leap a mud puddle
and please let us know what's on its other side.

Obsessively insane? If I told you, you'd know
everything. And then the bold lies come out—like,
Overturn them hot galaxies! We'd see the results

if you'd come clean. Whatever else happens
we'd make our precise plans for reconnecting.

Stretch out an empty hand, seek forgiveness:
the gnarled willow tree by your river begs salvation.
(A result of twisted motives may quite be like ataxia.)

What happens when you become lighter-than-air? All
of a sudden you gain perspective and can break away.

Any three or perhaps more interlocked rings suggest
someone's brilliant counterexamples in topology;
occasionally, science addresses all solids and substances.

Fingerlings—they are well-trained and eager
but see what happens when parrs grow old?

Oil will spill out onto the clean carpet and then
the landlord will evict us and we'll have to find
shelter under the old oak trees in the schoolyard.

Snowman / R. J. Keeler

A long fallow stretch. . .several gilded apple trees;
obscurants be dammed or underseen.

After lunch, all the steeple bells go off; go
visit all your afterlives, although *not* black river-seas that stream onto
black shores. Ebony charcoal coal, onyx pitch, inky cheerless bruises.

Another dreadful blonde joke unmasked—but the sea
was seen as angry that day, rarely seen nice and fresh.

Who deserves to see an underside of a silvery night moth?
Quadratures slink out to play the rainbows; hot dahlias
spawn and die, all very natural, expected, allowed.

Plato's Cave Redux

Doesn't that mindless horde know it's hopeless?
They can't go back; they have seen venal Truth,
and that Truth—well, it's set to set them free.
Please, stop your pitiful crawling toward that cave!

Pity, they can't bury what's been half-seen of Truth;
those shameless, unchained, multivalent lemmings
know no better life then back inside some smoky cave.
So go, new-minted Philosophers, return to ignorance;

you'll be chained again—poor imprisoned lemmings—
to unlearn that shadows on a wall are *not* a real book.
Go waddle in hot suns before slumping back to ignorance.
Fruitless! Not learn a thing you hadn't already grasped.

Against a tasty dinner, you'll digest *shadow* out from *book*
and recall: all things—beans, sun—are quarried out of stars.
All awkward and alike—to darkness, you who never grasped
that punting tasty multicolors reverts you to black and white.

You retrenching Philosophers—no guidance from any star,
nor truth from any book, will henceforth set you free;
by despising the outside melting sun, you revert to b&w;
your fate is hard and sealed; escape would be quite tasteless.

The Only Color of White

White is only a springboard for flowers—
fate is a pale crystal only by comparison.
If white disappears, what takes its place,
and will it ever matter? Beautiful, beautiful.

There was a time I could win by splashing midnight
black over some, and every, scene, but turn
white inside-out now, I'll take what's left, I'll
bundle it up into a tiny ball to sell it.

Then encryption the cleanest path forward;
could there be anything else in a land
of only white? So, hove to, luff those white sails,
they can double as shrouds.

Turn white inside out and smell it, what's it like?
What if, just if, an entire unknown universe
went stark white in one strong, malignant instant?
That sound of all light coming towards us so quickly.

This man on a white horse with a bow and arrow
represents War, is about to announce the Apocalypse,
the Last Judgement; wickedness
delivers its effects.

White is white; what splashes it
onto even more white shows faintly
as if everything were of color.

On Receiving an Author's First Book of Poems

Of course, of course, leaf through. Show interest.
But consider this hint:
start at the back (this may be done inconspicuously)
and from there page forward,
as the author undoubtedly placed
his most severely overworked pieces
at the front.

As you read each poem, ignore the first half.
This is superfluous material
which the author thought necessary
to ease you into his work.
In his next book, be assured he will have learned.
Each poem will leap immediately
right into the middle of what is happening,
on the assumption that you desire to be challenged.

As for utility, reckon
that when held firmly in the dominant hand,
spine down toward the fireplace,
if used vigorously, his book makes an effective fan
to spark slivers of creamy pine kindling
piled around red-smoldering paper.

For God's sakes stop!
Do not write your name on the bastard title page.
Put this book on a hall closet's top shelf
next to the silver wrapping paper
with green- and red-skewed tridents.
Take it down next November, wrap and send it to
Niece Andi with a nice card.

Perhaps I might suggest using this book as a vicious insect swatter.
But having spent the first five years of my childhood
among foreign coffee plantations, and the next seven
joyously on an equatorial coastline—
much of that time near the sea during dry season—
I have seen enough of such dispatching
to consider it offensive.

There Are No Found Poems, Just Found Rags, Bones

Use any old poem—perhaps even one
you found just this afternoon—to mop up spilled
gravy from your dinner table, or clean dust
off the venetian blinds, or to dry the cat
after its forced bath.

Conversely, go read a tattered rag like it was any common ode or lyric.
Ask, what was that rag originally—jeans, a curtain, a bathing suit?
Ask, where had it traveled? How did it get so shattered, so unraveled?

Perhaps that rag
    you picked up out of the discard bin
    is the very last rag,
    like the very last poem.
Or just like any commonplace bone.

Unknown Unknowns

It takes two to make an accident, said Jordan—that last, kicky feint from Wizards of the Coast
    Previously
    Sadness

Bludgeoned by a dozen lost opportunities for hot, free, juicy sex—we drove a 1945 Willys jeep
    Lineaments
    Love

Three round, gray stones in an exact, straight line—third-wave ska originated in the punk scene
    Athenaeums
    Snow

In Thomas Cole's paintings, tree stumps are negative and ugly—depicting the great, high truth
    Rogue wave
    Aloof

Native savages could never comprehend (i.e., visualize) Columbus's ships at anchor offshore
    Blueberries
    Weakness

For fifteen minutes, I aqua-lunged underwater—a six-foot barracuda following me just behind
    Pellucidar
    Spring

Rome's desolation (e.g., temples in ruins)—a higher purpose, without structured intellectual allegory
    Cassegrain reflector
    Lily-livered

Descendants of the Sun God sinter ephemera—Sarah Silverman sluts off, *My butthole itches*
    Entrained
    Irrelevant

Snowman / R. J. Keeler

A long, long time ago, before content—*It will flame out, like shining from shook foil*— rescue pod
    Lopsided
    Buttery

Curtains of White

White fog over the span of waters.
Everything slows way down.
Curtains of white.
      Somewhere off to leeward on earth's flat-grey plain stands
a wide-open,
apparently bare-naked-empty,   all-white room.

Inside that room, on the back wall, a door's outline—
      also white—covered and draped with a pure, white curtain.
Through that first door, past that first curtain, encounter a second empty

      room and then another, and then more doors and more curtains—
everything all-white.

All those white fluttering curtains,
      they ripple and slide about; and, if our gaze were to avert,
even for one split-second, they can transmute
      into gauzy souls of the best-known kind: souls white and
fluttering, not counterfeit like mine has become.

I remember times when there was not any so-called *I*—
      that *I* was all tricks, all post-magical tricks;
so whatever *I* was there, was beaten and beaten again and
      then beaten some more, until its *I*-ness's ethereal matter
      glowed hot-white.
And, therefore, one or the other, or something else entirely,
      came forward to make claims on the strange *I*-ness

Now, past lost indulgences, I firmed my hope up, then doubled it.
      Now, my hope is gossamer-made and gossamer-sewn.
Now, my hope, like a white curtain, is a feather of hot light.
      Like a fiercer ember,
around me all the oceans have come to fore, to force.

      I am opened wide now by many kinds of wild forces.
I am never to become a seer. I have very little *I* left anymore, am almost
no longer
I. But at end of day what does *I* matter?

Snowman / R. J. Keeler

If I were a bird, I would neither peck nor fly; I would dance up
> to orbit
>> the slender spires of my vanishing *I*-ness.

And, at end, like a bird, I'd soar to white, through, beyond
> pure white into that thickest whiteness—but I am
there no longer. *I* have been dismissed,
> have become disintegrated, am particulates.

Then time, so very elastic and white, springs in and out, beats like wings.

The First Horse

I, First Horse, a being of split-open
universes, am unexampled, recherché.

My human blood-brother, Chrysaor,
(Poseidon our sire, Medusa our dam)

remains behind to spawn his brood.
But damn all these empty, virgin

plains—so, Athena, Zeus, give me wings.
Am I not the nixed curse-horse? Am I

not First Horse, that ferried Thalia,
Calliope, Urania, Euterpe—Delphic

muses—down to humble *méritants*?
Or a workhorse to gods, dispatched

to fetch thunderbolts, to ferry
Olympus's up-riders? I'm pained

to be so rare—once, I even prayed
for divers kin, for ceaseless life.

Now, Zeus, I've served thee well.
Above I spy The Bull, The Ram,

Canis, and The Sea-Goat.
I yearn to fly once more only; so

I beg, perform your catasterism.

(The high moral tone)

The high moral tone that he used in the bequest speech was judged to be insincere and moreover was received by all the audience consisting of family and attorneys and friends as borderline insubordination but regardless of the tone we all had to agree with each other that it was delivered the language not the tone with exquisite precision and correctness in addition the grammar was absolutely flawless to the point where during the speech there were at least three phrases that stopped my attention cold and for them I had to focus and quickly in the moment form a mental image of the sentence in question and ask is that correct wow I must have been using that word incorrectly all these years furthermore the content to my ears and listening mind sounded expertly well-crafted and even a bit rhetorical one got the sense that the speaker had labored over the speech well into the night before he gave it and had gone over it in the privacy of his study again and again asking himself what do I want the audience to conclude from this speech and how therefore do I guide them invisibly to that desired conclusion at the end of this bequest speech or maybe an hour afterwards after the show of hands and the signing of documents I began to realize that the whole affair was so very well-scripted and designed as to be underhanded and to manipulate us all into innocent little lambs acceding to the agendas of the speaker but by then it was too late

We Must Pray the Prayer That Knows No Words

     Michael said:
Stories are but vessels—just like little ships. But
no handful of your stories will ever lead us
to a single, solid truth. And truth
only begins in a lie.

     Then he continued:
Good friend, take note; underneath your ever-clever stories—
which even you term sordid or empty—
do, surprisingly, lie brighter and deeper truths;
none of your counter-lies there.

     And went on:
Those deeper truths—they consist of, what?
Is it some story, or a fact, or a truth?
No, my friend—truths themselves are made out of one thing only,
a thing known precisely as myth.

     He noted:
But even these things that are myths—
they find themselves,
if you dig deeper, to be grand wrappers
around holy, base prayers.

     And added:
Like little gifts to us, by their secret means, prayers and
myths hold up our deepest, holiest notions.
Myths obligate us into play, to silences,
to incredible essences of all kinds. Prayers deliver us, he said.

     And at end Michael stated:
Smooth seas never made
too many good sailors.

Wolves howl to rally a pack, or to attack prey;
                whales whistle to collect a pod, to mate.
Animal scents drift along streams of warm air—
                chemistry, all just base chemistry.

Habitude

Foxes kneel to their half-light as
if they were searching quietly for
some highest point in their galaxy,
some point where soft dreamlines
occasionally, colorlessly, accumulate.

So, pick one dreamline up by its edge;
see, so like our tasty chocolates. Do
love the shy ones first, next the bolder
ones, even one foxy, little inside-
out dreamlets. Excellent! Now pool

that canon's flimsiness into combust
lots—their nebulae won't care, won't
miss; angry foxes can't tear them apart,
are too insubstantial to feed their kits,
which, when found at last, displace

sound-frogs; they may try to jump over.
There, you women of grace and dignity,
who nevertheless live like fey animals!
Your false-pink death mask just cannot
tamp a vixen muse down to priest holes.

Those dreamlines—a good run, hey?

Nemawashi

*—in Japanese, literally translates as going around the roots:
digging around the roots of a tree to prepare it for transplant.*

If a poem were a tree—articulated, breathing,
its trunk sturdy and anchored—a line of thought
that towered over the landscape, its outer surface spiraled and alive,
its cap profuse with life-giving energy;
underneath, its root ball a nutrient-gathering tangle,
cross-connected and enmeshed to its nurturing body, the bold earth.

If a poem were a tree, we would proceed with utmost respect
for its uniqueness,
for its inextinguishable right to exist.
Each day of the year we would honor our tree, slowly,
endlessly circling around and around it—imploring
its trunk, roots, and leaves,
then pause until we had lifted out a thin circle of sound
or a few small grains of crumbly intent, or a meaning.

If a poem were a tree, as we worked over the course of a year
we would always honor it. At the close of each workday
we would wish it well
and pray the tree would become suited
and pleased with its future home to-be.

As we deconstructed that tree, out of much care and affection
we would fashion scaffolding—forms and footings—around its base
to guarantee its vitality, health, and humor.

After a year of meticulous excavation, at the point
that the tree was grounded into its home soil
through only the thinnest stalk of sensibility,
we would convene and impanel a special ceremony—a festive,
congratulatory event—
and at its end intone aloud, once only,
the poem's very last phoneme.

After that, our poem would be free
to lift out of its own ground and skillfully cross
onto its new home.

Oh, That Heartstrike

Often at night I hear soft winds outside.
At next morning, rain confirms itself
to a few city blocks, and five or six bridges,
where there seems nothing to be afraid of.

Still, vagabonds hang out, bottles of cheap wine;
soft music spills over bridge steps and cornices,
ragtime girls gather, dip and stretch, whirl left—
I can never hear the melody from so far away.

The dancers pass behind each other slowly
and thoughtfully, as if translucent, as if half-real
silhouettes who sample foreign lives into tiny
exercises, into forms and strictures, historic

imprintings and dragoonings—into slipstreams,
essential concavities. Those translucent dancers
this instant reprise on that far-off bridge like
an isolated starburst of gauze or windiness.

Tired finally, their forms now descend into
numerology, into where, in Chaldean, a single
felt heartstrike is seven but in Pythagorean
is eight; so thereafter, Chaldeans may never

cause to muse about esoteric wanderings. My
lonesome, insubstantial doves, past dancing
on bridges, please, be done, do slam shut
the door. Next, my mind goes out to far seas,

to rogue waves, to million-fathom deeps—
the pressure down its farthest corners.
But, still more corners, more angles, veil
upon veil to be seen and folded neatly.

Notes

- "Airlock": "Pressure Drop"—words and music by Frederick Hibbert, Copyright© 1969 Beverley's Records Ltd., Copyright Renewed, All Rights Controlled and Administered by Universal— Songs of Polygram International, Inc. All Rights Reserved. Used by Permission. Reprinted by Permission of Hal Leonard LLC.
- "Birds": Basic models of bird-flocking behavior are controlled by three simple rules.
- "Black Swan": "Black Swan Theory," https://en.wikipedia.org/wiki/Black_swan_theory.
- "Calling Something by a Different Name": Dolphins have been found to have signature whistles, unique to each specific individual. In Catholic exorcism, a demon cannot be expelled until an exorcist has forced the demon to give up its name. "To get a meaning of a name like Philip, one must go back to its original Greek version, *Philippos*, which means 'lover of horses'" (Encyclopedia Britannica).
- "Death of a Horse at High Altitude": During the 1960 Rome Olympics, an American horse named Markham had to be destroyed in-flight because he panicked and went berserk, endangering everyone's safety. Most planes used for horse transport have a loaded gun onboard, and the pilots in command can authorize euthanasia in the event of an emergency.
- "Divinity of Christ": The lines "the search for truth sustains / the man—the quest for truth, a pathless / land" are from Jiddu Krishnamurti. "neti neti"—a Sanskrit expression from the Upanishads.
- "Epitaph for Preconsent Decree AT&T": Peter Temin, with Louis Galambos, *The Fall of the Bell System: A Study in Prices and Politics*. Stanza five, after Berryman's Sonnet #37.
- "Head End Hop Off": A method of traffic engineering whereby a system's calls are completed by using long-distance facilities directly off the final trunk-line switch. "Telephone Tribute," http://www.telephonetribute.com/glostele.htm#h
- "Insufficient Opportunity": William Mulvihill, *Sands of the Kalahari*.
- "Modesty Blaise, John Galt: A Forgotten Love Story": Peter O'Donnell, Crime Time, June 29, 2002, http://www.crimetime.co.uk/girl-walking-the-real-modesty-blaise/

- "Of Dark or Bright Forces": Joseph Campbell (and others), *The Hero's Journey*. *Avalokiteśvara*, the Buddhist Bodhisattva. *Kali*, Hindu destroyer of evil forces.
- "Oh, Make-Believe": Douglas Hofstadter, *Gödel, Escher, Bach*.
- "On Receiving an Author's First Book of Poems": The half title or bastard title is a page carrying nothing but the title of a book—as opposed to the title page, which also lists subtitle, author, publisher and edition. I spent the first five years of my childhood in Conveñcion and then the next seven in Coveñas, Colombia, S.A.
- "On the Occasion of the Incarceration of the Assistant State Attorney General's Wife for Making over One Hundred Threatening Telephone Calls to Her Neighbor": "Woman Charged in Eerie Threats by Phone to Family," Seattle Times, Dec. 5, 1991. C. S. Lewis, *That Hideous Strength*. Eric Eddison, *The Worm Ouroboros*. *Scats*: fecal droppings. Robinson Jeffers, "Age in Prospect," "a creature progressively / Thirsty for life will be for death too."
- "Pain Is Pleasure's Principle": After "Thurso's Landing" by Robinson Jeffers: ". . . No life / Ought to be thought important in the weave of the world, whatever / it may show of courage or endured pain. / It owes no other manner of shining. . . . / but to bear pain; for pleasure is too little, our inhuman / God is too great, thought is too lost." Also, Jeffers: "He has joy, but joy is a trick in the air; and pleasure, but pleasure is contemptible; / And peace; and is based on solider than pain." Also, The Beatles, "Girl," "Was she told when she was young / that pain would lead to pleasure?"
- "Plato's Cave Redux": The Ekphrastic Challenge image that inspired this poem:

Photo/Image by Nicolette Daskalakis,
www.nicolettedaskalakis.com
- "Ross Dam": Dedicated to Seattle City Light. Based on an observation by my friend DB.
- "Snake" and "Snake Medicine": Inspired by Brewster Ghiselin's poem "Rattlesnake."
- "Spell Check": Bergen-Belsen and Majdanek were Holocaust death camps. Peter Hayes, *Why?: Explaining the Holocaust*.

- "The Antithesis of Magic": The Karlowitz family were neighbors and co-workers. When, on vacation to either North or South Dakota, they walked into a motel and flipped on the light switch, they were all killed in a resulting explosion; a gas leak had filled the motel room. *Gale* is Gale Porter Kyle Delaney and *Jim* is Jim Byrum. I participated in the search for this suicided woman, dead in the marsh, while I was at Submarine Service boot camp at Charleston, S.C.
- "The First Horse": In Greek mythology, *catasterism* is the transformation of a hero or mythological creature, after death, into a star or constellation.
- "The Invention of the Snowman": ". . . except as a villain, as Lucifer stole her soul and fully corrupted her into demonic succubus. . . ." https://hero.fandom.com/wiki/Beatrice_(Dante%27s_Inferno)
- "The Right of the Sun to Die": As a kid, I learned how to splice 35mm films running on old gear-and-sprocket movie projectors.
- "The Twice-Born": Ghosts have been appearing in photographs almost since the time George Eastman introduced celluloid film for portable cameras during the 1880s.
- "There Are No Found Poems, Just Found Rags, Bones": Yeats, "The Circus Animals' Desertion," and the last line, "In the foul rag-and-bone shop of the heart."
- "Twinned Sides": Joni Mitchell, "Both Sides Now," "I've looked at clouds from both sides now / From up and down, and still somehow / It's cloud illusions I recall / I really don't know clouds at all."
- "Unknown Unknowns": *Wizards of the Coast* is an American publisher of games, primarily based on fantasy and science fiction themes. "It will flame out, like shining from shook foil," Gerard Manley Hopkins, "God's Grandeur." *Pellucidar* is a fictional Hollow Earth invented by American writer Edgar Rice Burroughs.
- "We Must Pray the Prayer That Knows No Words": Based on Michael Meade's 2017 lectures on mythology; his organization is called *Mosaic Voices*.

Snowman / R. J. Keeler

About the Author

R. J. (Robert) Keeler was born in St. Paul, Minnesota, and grew up in the jungles of Colombia. He holds a BA in Mathematics from North Carolina State University, an MS in Computer Science from the University of North Carolina-Chapel Hill, an MBA from UCLA, and a Certificate in Poetry from the University of Washington.

An Honorman in the U.S. Naval Submarine School, he was Submarine Service (SS) qualified.

He is a recipient of the Vietnam Service Medal, Honorable Discharge, and a Whiting Foundation Experimental Grant.

Mr. Keeler is a member of IEEE (technological society), AAAS (scientific society), and the Academy of American Poets. He is also a former Boeing engineer.

Mr. Keeler currently lives on Vashon Island, Washington. He is a minor Luddite, thus can only be contacted by email at: ncsu.snowman@gmail.com.

The Invention of the Snowman is his second published book of poetry. His first was *Detonation* (Wipf and Stock, 2020).

Manor House
905-648-4797
www.manor-house-publishing.com

www.ingramcontent.com/pod-product-compliance
Lightning Source LLC
Chambersburg PA
CBHW071849070526
44583CB00016B/1612